Secrets and Surprises

The Chateau Series Book 3

EMMA SHARP

DEDICATION

To my Family.

ACKNOWLEDGMENTS

Editor - Lynn Worton

Cover design - Sarah Jane Design

Web - www.emma-sharp-author.com

Email - info@emma-sharp-author.com

1

What's that noise? Abruptly sitting up from a deep sleep makes the room spin. I'd almost forgotten that I'm pregnant, nearly eight weeks now. My mouth feels parched, like the earth in summer. I can't believe I've slept all night. There it is again, a low rumbling noise. After draining the glass of now tepid water at my bedside, I make my way over to the window and pull the flimsy voile curtain to one side. Xavier. He never stops. What were the words Enzo used to describe him? *That man's like a machine.* Yes. Man and machine, working together. He's sat on the old tractor cutting the lawns if you can call them that.

The grass is beginning to take on a yellowish tinge, and it's only May. When I arrived last year at the end of July, the grass was knee-high and dead. How does it recover? Nature is truly amazing. Wow! I can't believe I've been here nearly a year, so much has changed. Where has the time gone? I know I've changed; truly changed, and now I'm at the beginning of my next journey. The most significant change I'll ever face. Parenthood.

I wish my mum and gran were still alive. I have no relatives, not even a sibling. I place a protective hand over my abdomen and whisper, "Sweet Pea, it's just you and me." I raise my eyes and look back out of the window, and I know that's not true. Sweet Pea has a father. A good man. And Alice, yes, a grandmother too, and a half-brother, Gus. A ready-made family, amazing people. When should I tell them? Not yet, at twelve weeks, I think. I search through the knowledge in my brain, trying to remember my brief stint in obstetrics. Yes, the first twelve weeks, that's when most miscarriages happen. Miscarriage. The word sticks in my throat. Ironic. A few weeks ago, I decided that I wanted a termination, and here I am now, worried about having a miscarriage. Get a grip, Laura.

A wave of nausea washes over me. Food, I need food. In the kitchen, I find a tin of shortbread that Alice brought over, not the healthiest of breakfasts but I rather fancy some with a cup of weak black tea. The thought of milk makes my stomach turn. Hmm, our milk is raw, pregnant women and young children aren't supposed to drink raw milk, are they? What about Gus? I'm sure that they weaned him on it. Research required.

I somehow lose the next two hours buried deep inside the internet. How did my parents and grandparents manage without it? Where did they get their information from? With only a few pamphlets and books, they couldn't have been very well informed; what a very different world we inhabit now.

The beginning of December, that's when Sweet Pea should arrive. It seems a long way off, but I know it will pass quickly. Not only do I have to prepare for the arrival of a new baby, but I also have a business to run. I'm going to need some help. And I need to talk to Xavier. I'm clueless as to how to proceed. "Xavier, congratulations, you're going to be a father again!" Somehow it sounds wrong. Does he want this baby? He's given me no indication as to how he feels about it. I can't put it off any longer, so I send him a text.

Can you call in when you have time, please?

I count to sixteen before I receive his reply.

Are you okay? Do you need me now?

Poor Xavier, he's been hanging around all morning, looking for jobs to do near the Chateau. I know he's worried about me.

Whenever you're free, it's not urgent.

Ten minutes later I hear his footsteps crunching on the gravel, here goes. I turn my back to the door and busy myself preparing lunch. Xavier must be hungry. He asks as he enters the room, "Laura, 'ow are you?"

I wave my arm towards the food on the table. "Hello, Xavier. I'm okay, thank you for coming, help yourself."

His eyes don't stray from my face as he makes his way over to wash his hands. "Do you 'ave to go back to ze 'ospital? I will take you."

Hesitating, I look down at the condensation forming on the outside of the glasses of ice-cold water. "No, well, not yet anyway. Xavier… please sit down. I've got something to tell you."

Robotically, he plonks himself on a chair at the table, and I take my place opposite him.

"What is it?" He asks.

"Xavier, I didn't take the medication… I've, erm, decided to keep the baby." His eyes widen, and his mouth drops open. Is that a positive or negative reaction? I don't know. "Say something," I add, lowering my eyes.

He jumps up and is at my side in a flash. "We are 'aving ze baby? Is zat what you want?"

"Yes, yes, I am. Perhaps we should have discussed it together — and I understand if you don't want to be involved…"

"You zink I don't want ze baby? I am ze fazer, and yes, I want ze baby," he says, getting louder with every word. "Laura, I will do whatever you want. I can be 'ere every day, I can sleep 'ere if you want…"

"That's generous of you, thank you, but I don't need you to sleep here. Apart from morning sickness, I'm okay, and that will pass. Let's not tell anyone for a few more weeks. I, erm, understand that you will want a DNA test doing, seeing as it was so soon after Enzo…"

"If you say zat it is mine, zen I believe you," he says, with a look of complete trust.

"People will gossip — they will assume it's Enzo's child," I sigh.

"Well, unless it's born wiz ze ginger 'air and a beard, zey can go to hell!"

"I promise you; it won't be," I say, trying to sound upbeat. Is it even possible to have a safe DNA test done during pregnancy? I expect so, something else to research. But I already know it can't be Enzo's child, so I'm not worried about that. However, I am concerned about everything else. The birth — I'm not looking forward to the prospect of passing something the size of a watermelon, I've witnessed several torn perinea. It's not something I want to experience for myself!

"You are miles away, what is going on in your 'ead?" He asks, taking hold of my hand over the table.

"Erm, I'm just thinking how it's all going to work…"

"Don't. We will all 'elp. Mama will be so excited. She will do ze childcare," he says.

"Yes, but we are supposed to be growing the business; we need her to work alongside Rose and Yvette."

"It's early days, let's take one day at a time. Now, what do you need me to do today?" He asks.

"I want you to continue as normal, that's what I intend to do."

"Okay, but promise you will not do too much, all you 'ave to do is ask and I will 'elp. Yes?"

"Yes Xavier, I will ask when I need your help and thank you for being supportive."

"But of course, I will support you! You know 'ow I feel about you, yes? And, you 'ave to go back to ze doctor," he says, standing while performing an exaggerated shrug, so typical of him. I know I can depend on him and Alice. I already think of her as my surrogate mother. An uncomfortable thought pops into my head – doesn't that make Xavier my surrogate brother? Yes, I have feelings for him, but I need time to discover what they are. Was my alcohol-fuelled one-night stand only lust? Or was it a rebound thing? I had recently just walked away from Enzo after all. I'm so confused.

2

I try to continue as usual but find myself avoiding Alice, making as many excuses as I can to not visit the farmhouse, finding jobs elsewhere on the estate; especially when I know that she's coming to the Chateau to use the ovens for the catering side of things. Only three weeks to go now until I reach twelve weeks, then we will need to tell her. I've plucked up courage and have an appointment with the doctor this afternoon, not something I'm looking forward to doing. I've told Xavier that I'm going to the library. Otherwise, he would have insisted that he came with me.

I walk into the dingy waiting room and come face to face with Yvette. I knew it was a possibility, but I had hoped that she might be busy baking with Alice and Rose. "Hello Mademoiselle Mackley, take a seat, the doctor won't be much longer," she says.

I smile and nod before sitting in the corner to wait, listening to an antique clock slowly ticking the seconds away. Five agonising minutes pass before a voice calls me into the small surgery. I step through the door, then close it behind me. "Hello again, what can I do for you?" The same doctor asks, not taking his eyes from his desk.

"Hello, I'm nine weeks pregnant and would like to book in with your maternity services please," I say, repeating the same sentence out loud that I've sat and rehearsed over and over to myself.

The doctor's head pops up with surprise. I appear to have his attention now. "Oh, erm, that's good news," he replies, slowly regaining his composure. "Congratulations." It doesn't take him long to scribble a note on a piece of paper, then looking back up at me with a warm smile, "If you give this to my receptionist, she will make the necessary arrangements for you." Déjà vu! This time, it doesn't feel like the walk of shame as I leave his tiny room and head back out to find Yvette.

She takes the note from me, and her face softens, "Congratulations, would you like to use the local hospital or go back to the city?"

"The local hospital please," I say, then hesitate before continuing, "I haven't told my staff yet…"

Yvette interrupts, "Your secret is safe with me." She, of course, has no idea that it's Xavier's baby. Both of our heads turn instinctively to the door as it opens. I don't believe it. It's Alice. Shit!

"Oh, Alice, what are you doing here?" I ask without thinking.

"I was just wondering the same; I thought you were going to the library."

"Erm…" I stutter.

"Mademoiselle Mackley just needed me to sign some papers about the new job, I asked her to pop in here as I'm working this afternoon," Yvette interrupts, saving the day.

"Yes, I'm just on my way into town, do you need anything picking up?" I ask.

"Actually, yes. We're short of almonds. They'll be cheaper on the market than they are in the village, that will save Xavier a trip. I'm only ordering my repeat prescription. You could have dropped it off for me If I'd known you were coming," Alice says. Phew, that was too close for comfort! But now I do have to go into town.

Like last time, it's busy, lots of mums with babies and young children. There probably always has been, but they weren't previously on my radar. I stroll through the market.

Many of the stalls are now packing up, but I manage to find some almonds for Alice then continue wandering the streets, passing the pharmacy where I had my unfortunate encounter with Enzo. Thankfully, I haven't heard from him since. I make my way into the small department store, Jenny's favourite shop, and browse through their new summer range. I pick up a pair of canary yellow capri pants that I like and drape them over my arm as I continue browsing. Wandering around idly, I look up after almost bumping into someone, and realise I'm now in the baby department. A white crib dressed in yellow accessories jumps out at me, and I'm drawn towards it by some unstoppable force. "May I help you?" Asks an immaculately dressed woman, slightly older than me. She must be a member of staff, as she's wearing a name tag on the jacket.

"Erm, I'm only browsing, thank you," I say, embarrassed, and move on quickly, forcing myself not to look at the cute teddies and

endless racks of baby clothes. Standing at the
check-out I come to my senses – why do I
think I'm going to need a pair of tight-fitting
capri pants? I'll be wearing tents in a few
weeks! Turning tail, I replace them and walk
out of the store. It still hasn't sunk in that I'm
having a baby! It's surreal. On my way back to
the car I'm side-tracked by a fantastic aroma
— chocolate. Coming to an abrupt halt, I scan
the nearby shops. I'm standing outside a shop
called Bon-Bon's, and it smells yummy.
Resistance is futile, and I enter into an
Aladdin's cave; it's a kaleidoscope of colours,
and my eyes don't know where to look first.
Salted caramel truffles, chocolate and ginger
fudge, crystallised fruit jellies, and that's only
the start. I spy a chocolate fountain in the
corner and help myself to a baby-pink
marshmallow, dipping it into the dark, shiny
liquid and then savour the fantastic flavour as
it melts across my tongue; bitter and sweet,
chewy and smooth. Decadence, and I want
more. I'm about to dip a piece of fruit and nut

nougat in next when the assistant walks up to me and makes a show of clearing his throat.

"The fountain is for display purposes only, madam," he says rather curtly. Embarrassed, I realise what I've done and apologise profusely, offering to pay for the pieces I've wantonly consumed. "Do you intend to make a purchase, madam?" he continues.

"Oh yes," I say, scrambling for one of the boxes next to the alluring display in which to place my selections. What was I thinking? I exit the shop with three boxes of hand-made chocolates, and by the time I reach home I've gorged my way through one of them. Before long, I begin to feel sick; it serves me right for eating the whole box!

3

I pick up my tablet to check my emails, as I do every morning, but today, I allow myself to drift; it's the start of week ten. I click on the icon that takes me straight to my baby calendar and satisfy myself by reading the developmental stage of my pregnancy for the week. Sweet Pea is now the size of a strawberry and is beginning to get hair and fingernails. Wow, she's growing fast. I should have put on a few pounds too, that would be the chocolates! I have noticed I'm feeling hungrier now; except first thing in a morning – hopefully that should pass in a few more weeks. Xavier had evidently been doing some research of his own, as he turned up with a packet of ginger biscuits for me yesterday. He knows I'm going to the hospital to book in next week, but I've asked him not to come with me. I think he's a little disappointed, but I don't want Alice to suspect anything. He'll be too busy anyway, as he's collecting the puppies tomorrow, Patch, Pepper, and Freckles; I can't wait to see them. I would love to have them here at the Chateau, but Xavier is probably right. I will spoil them. '*Zey are working dogs, not pets,*' he insists. I suppose they've got to get used to living in a kennel outside. I think the best thing I can do is to keep my distance from them. He will be selling them anyway, once they have learned their role as truffle dogs from their father, Shadow.

Closing the app, I go back to my emails. There are more bookings for the campsite and a couple of enquiries for weddings. Oh, and an inquiry for a vintage car rally. They want to stop for what they call a 'lunch halt' and do a test of some type on the estate; whatever that means. It's not until summer, anyway. I'll ask Xavier, see what he thinks. Now, I'd better get on. I've got a guest staying in the Chateau for the next two nights; he'll be arriving soon.

"Monsieur Laurent. Welcome! May I get you some refreshments?" I ask as I show my guest into the hall. He's a little man, wearing a dark grey suit and tie.

"A cold drink, please," he says, placing a small, tatty, leather case on the floor.

"Would you like to sit in the drawing-room or outside on the patio?"

"Drawing-room, thank you."

"No problem. This way, please."

After showing him the way, I head to the kitchen for his drink, pouring him an ice-cold lemonade that Alice made earlier, then place the glass on a small tray with some cookies. He's sat in the window seat taking in his surroundings.

"Here we are," I say, placing the tray at his side.

"How many other guests do you have?"

"Oh, you're the only one just now. Some more will be arriving at the weekend, though."

"I will have gone by then," he adds, scribbling something down in a notebook.

"Are you here on business?"

"Sort of," he replies evasively.

"Well, if you have time, we have a small museum that you are welcome to visit, it's in the library; and plenty of information leaflets displayed in the hall." He nods and jots down some more notes. How bizarre. "There's a bell on the reception desk in the hall. Please ring when you're ready to be shown to your room. Will you require dinner this evening?" Again, he only nods, so I hand him a menu from the holder near the door. "Dinner is at 7 pm," I add before retreating to the kitchen. Hmm, he does seem a strange little man.

A short while later, the little bell rings in the kitchen, and I walk out into the hall to find Monsieur Laurent reading the noticeboard. "Do you have a fire escape?"

"Yes, yes, we do. You will find the fire notice on the inside of your bedroom door, explaining what to do in case of an emergency," I say, trying to make my smile look natural. What a strange question. "Would you like to follow me?"

"Could someone take my bag up for me, please?"

"Oh, is it heavy?"

"No."

Plastering a smile on my face, but inwardly grumbling, I pick up his small case, and he follows me upstairs, where I show him to his room at the back of the Chateau.

"Is this the bridal suite?"

"Erm, no. You booked a standard room, sir."

"May I see the bridal suite?"

"Certainly, it's not in use at the moment, follow me," I say. This man is definitely peculiar. "Here we are." He steps into the room then heads over to the ensuite and opens the door.

"It doesn't have a bath," he states.

"No, it has a luxury steam cabinet and shower, but all guests have use of the hot tub on the rear patio."

He doesn't reply but nods and walks briskly back to his room. As I'm about to leave him, he turns and says, "I have a nut allergy, and I'm gluten-free, will that be a problem?"

"No, sir, it won't, but it clearly states on my website to email or ring to discuss any dietary requirements in advance."

"So, it is a problem?"

"Not at all, but it will limit your choice. What would you like for dinner?" I ask, trying to remain patient.

"What have you got that is suitable?"

"I will return in a short while with a new menu for your food intolerances," I say, turning to leave this awkward little man alone in his room. I'm going to require Alice's help, and I'm trying to avoid her. I call her at the farmhouse.

"Hello, Alice, sorry to bother you. I have an awkward guest who has a gluten and nut allergy. What do you suggest?"

"Hmm, difficult. You get on the internet, and I'll come over to help you make something."

Twenty minutes later, I have printed a new menu for Monsieur Laurent, and Alice is busy preparing the options in the kitchen. "Why does he have to be so awkward?" I ask.

"It's not like you to be so irritable, Laura. Don't worry. We have it under control now," Alice says. Yes, she's right. I need to prepare for eccentric guests; this is good practice. "I'll ring Xavier and ask him to pick up some gluten-free flour. He'll have to go into town; there won't be any in the village," she adds.

"Will we need it?"

"Yes, if he wants pancakes or toast for breakfast. I'll make a few of each for you to keep in the freezer, you never know when you'll need them," Alice adds. She is amazing. What would I do without her?

The next morning, Monsieur Laurent arrives for breakfast, and I ask, "I trust you slept well?"

"Yes, thank you," he says, picking up the menu. "Oh, I wanted porridge, and it's not on here," he adds.

"Not a problem. I can make you some porridge, but I can't guarantee that the oats are from a gluten-free environment."

"Actually, I'll have fresh fruit and natural yoghurt. Do you have that?"

"Yes, we do. Would you like tea or coffee?"

"Decaffeinated coffee, please," he replies, with a smug expression on his face. What is his problem? It appears as though he's trying to be awkward on purpose! Another item for my shopping list.

"Of course, sir. I'll be back with it shortly," I head to the kitchen and return a few minutes later. "Here we are," I say, placing the cafetière on his table, hoping he won't realise it's not decaffeinated.

As I'm about to head back to the kitchen to prepare his breakfast, he asks, "Could you recommend a local walk that's not too strenuous?"

"Yes, the village isn't too far, and it's a pleasant walk, or you could explore the estate; would you like a map?"

"Yes, please," he replies, drinking his coffee without complaining; perhaps the caffeine might help him to walk quicker.

I receive a text from Xavier at lunchtime.

Zere is a strange man snooping about in ze vines.

No prizes for guessing who that might be.

If it's a short man wearing a grey suit, then it's our guest, Monsieur Laurent.

I wonder what he's doing.

Yes, zat is 'im.

Oh dear, perhaps he's lost.

Ask him if he requires any help, and Xavier, please be polite.

Perhaps I should go over there, Xavier is protective of his vines. Fifteen minutes later, Monsieur Laurent returns, looking a little dusty. "Monsieur Laurent," I say, "did you enjoy your walk? Would you like some lunch?"

"No, thank you. I'm going to my room to do some work," he replies, marching past me.

Oh dear, I hope Xavier didn't upset him.

A short while later, my phone rings. It's Monsieur Laurent. "I would like room service, please."

What? I've only just asked him if he'd like lunch, "Yes, Monsieur Laurent; what would you like to eat?" I ask as patiently as I can.

"I don't know what you have. You don't appear to have a room service menu."

I ask, "A salad or sandwich, perhaps?" Holding my breath while waiting for his reply.

"Yes, a chicken salad sandwich, no mayonnaise, and a cold beer please," he says then ends the call. Dutifully, I take the man his lunch and return to the kitchen to prepare for dinner; who knows what he'll request this evening!

The following morning after breakfast, Monsieur Laurent walks into the hall and asks to check out. I present him with the bill, which, thankfully, I'd prepared last night after he'd gone to bed, itemising the extras that he had ordered.

"Could someone bring my luggage down, please?" He asks rather matter-of-factly as his card transaction is processed.

"Certainly, sir," I smile, turning to climb the stairs once the card is approved. I return with the bag a short while later and hand it to him. With the bill already settled; he puts it on the floor.

He surprises me by asking, "Could I see the manager?"

"Monsieur Laurent, I am the manager."

"Don't you have any staff?"

"It's a small, family-run business. I don't need any assistance with only one guest," I reply. "Do you have a problem?"

"No, just a few things I'd like to discuss with you. Shall we go into the drawing-room?" I follow him in, wondering what on earth I've done wrong. "Do take a seat, Miss Mackley."

As I sit, I ask, "What can I do for you, Monsieur Laurent?"

"Firstly, I'm not Monsieur Laurent. My name is Simon Aris, and I'm a hotel inspector."

Oh, my God! Why didn't I realise? Valentina warned me that one was bound to arrive incognito. "Monsieur Aris, I trust you found my establishment satisfactory," I manage.

"I've frequented much worse - but I will be writing a report with some recommendations, which you will receive in due course."

"What type of recommendations?"

"Nothing major," he replies, standing and offering his hand, which I reluctantly shake. "Thank you for your hospitality." He then leaves and climbs into his car without looking back. I expect he's moving on to his next unfortunate victim.

4

I have to tell someone, but who? Xavier, he's going to collect the puppies today. It's only 9.20 am. Perhaps I'll catch him.

Have you set off yet?

I've probably missed him, never mind, I can tell him later. There's nothing he can do anyway.

No, I'm about to leave, do you need me?

What should I say now? Yes, Xavier, I do need you, I'm carrying your baby after all. But do I need him? My feelings are all over the place, one moment I feel invincible, ready to take on the world single-handed, and the next minute I'm feeling vulnerable and lonely. What should I do? My thoughts are interrupted by a gentle knock on the kitchen door. Xavier enters. "Laura, are you okay? You look pale."

"Yes, but I've just had a shock."

Closing the distance between us, he takes hold of my hands, "What is ze problem?"

"Would you believe it, our guest, Monsieur Laurent, turned out to be a hotel inspector?"

"Zut Alors! Zat was sneaky. I did not like 'im. What did 'e say?"

"Not a great deal actually, he said there was nothing major but will make a few recommendations. He's going to write a report and post it to us."

"Zere is nozing we can do now, why don't you come wiz me to collect ze puppies? It will take your mind off ze 'otel inspector." Mm, it would be fun, but do I want to sit next to Xavier for an hour? What can we talk about? "Come on," he says, taking my hand and leading me to his truck.

"Okay, but let's take my Yeti; it will be far more comfortable, and we can get three puppies in the back," I say, handing him the keys.

Xavier stops in the village. I turn and look at him when he opens the door, preparing to get out. "Where are you going?"

"To get you ze breakfast, I can 'ear your stomach rumbling." Five minutes later, he climbs back in and hands me a bag of pastries and a bottle of water, "You are eating for two now." I sit and watch the scenery go by while slowly nibbling my breakfast. "'Ave you been to ze doctor yet?"

I swallow a gulp of water and fold down the top of the brown paper bag while choosing my words carefully. "Yes, I have."

He turns his head towards me momentarily then looks back at the road. "Well, what did 'e say?"

"Not much really – Yvette has made me an appointment at the hospital."

His head swings back in my direction. "When? I will come wiz you."

I knew this would be a problem. "Xavier, I'll be okay on my own. They probably won't be doing anything, just lots of forms to fill in, I expect, and a blood test." By the time I've finished speaking, we have pulled onto a piece of rough land near a farm. "Oh, are we here already?"

"No, we need to talk," he says, turning to face me. He picks up my hand and places it on my abdomen, covering it with his big calloused hand, and continues, "Laura, zis is my baby too. I realise zis is not 'ow you imagined life to turn out, but I love our baby, and I want to love you too if only you will let me." I look into his kind eyes and begin to soften.

He's right, it is his child but are we a good fit? He's a good man for sure but is that enough? It's a foundation we could build from, but is that what I want? Perhaps it's not about what I desire anymore. It's about Sweet Pea. I'm taken back into the past as I remember Adam telling me about his grandmother. She found herself pregnant through no fault of her own and was contented or possibly even relieved to marry a local man. Aunt Mary was in a similar situation and was about to marry poor Henri before he died; killed during the war. But I want to marry for love and nothing else. Yes, this is Xavier's child, and I will not deny him the opportunity to be a father. A good father, that's what Sweet Pea needs.

I try to let him down gently. I lift my eyes from his hand, still covering our baby and run my tongue over my tingling lips. I resist the urge to kiss him and begin my short speech, "Xavier, you're right, this is not how I envisaged my life, but thank you. My appointment is in a few days. If you want to come then, you can, though I think you might be bored. However, I don't think I'm ready for a relationship just yet. Please, can we be friends for now?" His bright eyes cloud over with disappointment, but he recovers well. He only nods and smiles before starting the Yeti and pulling out onto the road. The next twenty minutes pass with both of us lost in our thoughts and emotions.

"'Ere we are," he says, turning off into a drive outside a charming cottage. As I get out of the car, Xavier is at my side, offering me his hand. I ring the doorbell, and the racket starts; yapping dogs. "Zat will 'ave to stop. I will not 'ave zem yapping like zat," he says.

The door opens, and Sara arrives with Pipi tucked under her arm, "Laura, Xavier, how lovely to see you; do come in." Once inside we're shown into a stunning conservatory at the rear of the cottage, with patio doors opening onto an immaculate garden. Sara opens a door leading into a modern kitchen where four cute puppies are clamouring for our attention. "Darlings! Darlings, come and meet your new mummy!" Sara says in a sickly-sweet voice. Xavier looks at me and rolls his eyes skywards. Oh dear!

"Zey will 'ave to learn some manners," he whispers to me while pasting a false smile on his face.

My heart melts instantly. The puppies are the cutest things I've ever seen. Little fluffy balls of caramel on short stubby legs, with oversized paws and ears that they've yet to grow into. How on earth are they going to become truffle dogs? The largest one greets me first and makes a puddle on the floor while wagging his short tail excitedly. "Oh, Patchy-watchy, that's not a very good first impression," Sara scolds, in a not very firm or loud voice. Patch looks back at her with limpid eyes and continues wagging his tail. I can't see a patch anywhere on his little body. I then glance over to the others who all look very much the same.

"How do you know its Patch?" I ask.

"Darling, I can tell them all apart; they all have small characteristics of their own. Patch is always the first on the scene. He is bold and fearless; the pack leader and always first to the food."

"Good, 'e should be easy to train," Xavier comments. The other three follow on behind and career across the floor, sliding in the puddle left by Patch. Another puppy picks up a piece of coloured rope and begins to run off in a different direction. The other three take off after him, making little growling noises as they try to take control of the rope. After much bickering Patch wins, and the others concede defeat. "Zat is definitely ze best dog. I might 'ave to keep 'im." Xavier whispers again.

The puppies continue with their rough and tumble games while princess Pipi sits serenely on a pink cushion keeping an eye on them. Sara disappears to get refreshments and Xavier chooses this moment to walk across and pick up Patch. He then produces a marker pen from his top pocket and draws a black dot on the dog's head. "Why have you done that?" I ask naively.

"So, I can identify 'im."

"What about the others?"

"In time I will know which dog will make it – but I 'ave a feeling about 'im," he says quietly.

"What will you do with the ones that don't succeed as truffle dogs?"

"I will make sure zey all succeed," he says as Sara returns with a tray laden with goodies.

Sara blubbers into a cerise tissue as Xavier lifts Patch, Pepper, and Freckles into the back of the Yeti. "Oh! I'm going to miss them so much; you will remember to give them the special puppy food that I've given you – won't you?" She says between sobs. I nod solemnly but can feel Xavier's disapproval radiating off him as he finishes placing the puppies in the vehicle. Once Xavier closes the tailgate, Sara stands back with Pipi under one arm and

Penny under the other. "Don't worry my little darlings, we will go and visit them soon," she then looks at me and continues, "Laura, I'll ring to arrange a play date for the puppies." Oh dear, how am I going to deflect this? I mumble incoherently and hastily climb into the front seat, avoiding Xavier's glower. Penny and Pipi are placed gently on the floor as Sara waves until we are out of sight.

Once out of the small village Xavier speaks first, "Zat woman is crazy, I don't want 'er anywhere near ze puppies again."

"It's going to be difficult, Xavier. It's obvious she adores them."

"Special puppy food – huh! Zey will 'ave whatever I catch."

"Xavier, they won't be able to deal with feathers, fur, and bones for quite some time; they'll choke."

"First, I will give zem only ze meat, cut up small. 'Ow do you zink dogs manage in ze wild?"

"Where are they going to sleep tonight? Aren't they going to miss their mother?"

"Zey will manage."

Oh dear, this is going to be difficult. I wonder if Shadow will be able to tell that they are his offspring, but I decide not to ask. The gentle Xavier of earlier has gone. Now he's a man on a mission.

5

Xavier parks at rear of the farmhouse and opens the tailgate. Three frightened little faces peer back at us. Bending, he scoops all three up in one arm and puts them on the floor.

Patch is the first one to move, he starts sniffing around the back yard and squats to do yet another wee. Xavier reacts instinctively, offering him a sliver of meat, saying, "Good boy. See, 'e is scent marking already." Pepper and Freckles eventually notice their new surroundings and follow Patch wherever he wanders. Patch spies the open door and boldly walks into the kitchen. The other two try to follow, but Xavier places a piece of wood across the doorway to stop them.

"Why can't they go in? That's favouritism." I say sharply.

"No, it's training. Zey can go in ze 'ouse when zey 'ave done ze wee. Zey 'ave to learn," he replies, nudging the two creatures towards the puddle that Patch has left. Pepper is next to perform and allowed inside. Poor Freckles looks around, bewildered, and begins to whimper.

"Oh, the poor thing…" I say, reaching down to the little puppy.

"Don't, 'e 'as to learn. You go inside. Mama 'as made ze lunch."

Reluctantly, I do as I'm asked and instantly rewarded with a fantastic aroma, cinnamon and chocolate; my stomach starts to rumble. I'm starving. "Alice, it smells divine, thank you," I say as I step over the piece of wood and walk into the kitchen. She rushes forward and places her arms around me in a giant bear hug, squeezing my very sore breasts into her ample bosom.

"Laura, if I didn't know better, I'd think you were avoiding me. How are you?"

"Mama, Laura is very busy wiv ze 'otel and campsite, just like you and Rose are wiz ze cooking," Xavier says, finally letting Freckles through the door.

"Oh, has he managed?" I ask, pointing to the small puppy now looking around the kitchen in trepidation. Xavier nods, and I sit and take a large slice of quiche off a plate on the table. Xavier looks at me and smiles, and I realise that I'm behaving out of character. Should I put it back down again? No, it's too late, and I'm ravenous. I take a massive bite of the delicious food, followed by another.

"Someone's hungry," Alice comments.

"Sorry Alice, I missed breakfast," I say, then proceed to tell her about Monsieur Laurent, alias the hotel inspector. I hear a low growl and look over to see Beau lift his head off the floor as Patch approaches him. "Oh no! Will he hurt him?" I ask, making my way over to the puppy.

"Sit down," Xavier orders, "'e 'as got to learn 'is place." Patch backs off and takes a wide berth around the big dog. Beau rests his head on his paw and continues with his nap. "See, ze lesson is learned." Pepper is the next to notice the big dog and walks towards him cautiously. Again, Beau repeats his warning growl which Pepper heeds, putting his little tail between his legs and retreating. So far, so good. Poor Freckles' sits near a kitchen cupboard and is looking around, somewhat bewildered with the whole situation.

Alice brings me up to speed with the catering side of the business. It appears to be going well, and Yvette seems to be settling in, helping out when needed. Our heads turn in unison as Beau lets out an angry snarl. I jump up and rush towards Freckles, who is continuing to wander towards Beau's well-chewed bone despite the warning shot across the boughs.

"Stop!" Xavier barks as I approach the hapless puppy, but I ignore his command and continue walking. "Laura, stop!" He repeats. "Ze only way ze stupid dog will learn is by making ze mistake."

Freckles fails to heed Beau's warning and the big dog leaps up and head butts poor Freckles across the floor. I can watch no longer and scoop up the poor creature into my arms. "Xavier, he's only a baby. Beau will hurt him!" I shout, checking the unfortunate thing for signs of injury. Alice steps forward and takes the bundle of fur from me, putting Freckles back on the floor.

"Xavier is right," she says, "he will only learn by making mistakes. Some lessons are harder to take than others, but he won't do that again in a hurry."

I can no longer stay to watch poor Freckles learn his necessary life skills. My maternal instincts are on hyperdrive, and I need to escape. "Thanks for lunch, I'll leave you to your charges. I need to service the room that the hotel inspector stayed in," I say, making my excuses and heading back to the Chateau.

As I go about my jobs, I can't stop thinking about Xavier. Will he 'train' our child in the same way? Gus seems to be a well-rounded individual, quite mature for his age, and he didn't have the benefit of a doting mother. But I know Alice adores him. Gus has been brought up to help wherever he can. He even taught me how to milk the goats. Most

children of his age back in Leeds are sat glued
to a gadget of some type. I saw that here, too,
on the train journey to Paris. Perhaps it's a
city thing. I wonder if children in the rural
parts of the United Kingdom are brought up
to be more like Gus? How will I bring my
child up? It's not something to which I've
given much thought. Will Xavier and I agree?
I'm sure he'll be much stricter than me. I dare
say that he or she will have me wrapped
around its little finger. I try to push the
thought to one side and concentrate on my
work. It's a long time until I need to worry
about that.

6

Week eleven, and it's my first hospital appointment — booking in, as it's called back home. I allow myself the weekly browse on the baby calendar app. Sweet Pea is now the size of a fig and has a placenta. She is also beginning to look more like a human with an oversized head. According to the app, I need to rub coconut oil into my abdomen to prevent stretch marks; now that's something I hadn't considered. Stretch marks. No more bikinis for me then! It also states that morning sickness should be coming to an end, and I should soon start to feel radiant. Right now, I'm exhausted. Every day seems like an effort. I've even been falling asleep after lunch, which isn't like me at all. It seems raging hormones are to blame. A pricking sensation starts in my neck and travels down my spine. I raise my eyes from the screen and turn to find Xavier stood behind me. He whispers, "Fascinating, isn't it?"

"How long have you been there?"

"Just arrived," he says, then asks, "are you ready?" After I nod, Xavier takes my car keys from me and gets in the driver's seat. We set off in silence, each in our little world. I wonder what's going on in his head. I'm thinking about the first scan, between eight and fourteen weeks. Will they count the one that I had in the city? I hope not.

Xavier breaks the silence, "What are you zinking?"

"That's weird. I was just wondering the same thing about you."

"Ah, but I asked first," he replies mischievously, as though we're a couple of teenagers playing spin the bottle.

The entrance to the hospital car park is nearing, so I say, "Well, I was wondering if they will do another ultrasound scan; seeing as I've technically already had one to confirm the dates."

"But of course, zey will! Zey will need to do many tests to check for various zings," he says, driving into the car park. He's done his research, I note. Even in the smaller hospital, parking is difficult, but we eventually find a space, and Xavier continues, "Zis is where Mama came after she 'ad ze stroke." The familiar surroundings were clearly bringing back unpleasant memories for him.

"She is an amazing woman; she was so determined to make a full recovery."

"Yes, zanks to you…"

"No Xavier, I had very little to do with her recovery. I only helped to keep her comfortable; she did the rest herself."

He hesitates, then takes my hand, pressing it against his lips for the briefest of moments. "Mama was inconsolable after it 'appened, we didn't know 'ow we would manage ze farm and care for Gus, zen you came along; like it was meant to be."

I decide not to remind him at this point that he took an instant dislike to me and that I considered him ill-mannered and belligerent. Instead, we walk in silence through the corridors; no lines painted on the floor this time.

"'Ere we are," he says, as we enter the antenatal department. There's not a self-check-in screen in view. Xavier walks briskly up to the reception desk and gives them my name, and we're instructed to sit in the small waiting room. I can't help but notice the vast differences between here and the new city hospital I visited last time. The walls are painted a patchy green and hung with old, fading prints, and the floor covered in grubby carpet tiles; quite a contrast.

A nurse calls my name as she walks towards us from the corridor opposite. Xavier stands quickly, taking my hand and propels me towards her. Once seated inside her small room, she explains the process. I have to complete a substantial pile of forms, followed by general observations, blood pressure, weight, and height; before being dispatched to pee in a plastic container. Next, she requests which tests I'd like to have.

"All of zem," Xavier interrupts.

"Could I have a list of the tests available, please?" I ask, after frowning at him. I listen to the options and ask for more information about the risks that each test carries and tell her that I would like to think about it. Xavier sighs in the corner, but I refuse to look at him; it's my decision. Yes, we can discuss the options, but ultimately, I decide.

"Do we 'ave a scan?" Xavier then asks. The nurse goes on to explain that we need to make a further appointment on the way out to come back for an ultrasound scan.

"Now, if you would please remove your clothes, the doctor will be in shortly to examine you," she says then leaves us alone.

I look at the door as it closes behind the nurse then back at Xavier, "Exactly which clothes do I need to remove?" Xavier only shrugs as he remains seated in his chair. Looking over my shoulder, I notice a curtain pulled across part of the room. Standing, I go and investigate, relieved to see that an examination bed is screened off behind the curtain. Xavier isn't going to have a ringside seat. He stands to follow, but I hold up my hand, "Please, stay where you are."

Once behind the curtain I remove my jeans and top and lay down on the couch, pulling a towel over myself. I hear the door open a short while later, and a man's voice, introducing himself to Xavier. The doctor then arrives behind the curtain and repeats his introduction for me.

"Everything appears to be going well," he says, after gently prodding my abdomen. "Do you have any questions?" My hormone-soaked brain can think of nothing, so he leaves me to get dressed.

"There, nothing to worry about," I say as we make our way back to the car, with an appointment for a scan next week.

"Good. We need to discuss ze tests. You should 'ave zem all, yes?"

"Xavier, that wasn't much of a discussion, and I haven't decided yet. I need to do some more research."

"I 'ave done ze research already. All of ze tests are good for ze baby."

"Okay, let's go home and look at the internet and then decide together," I say. Trying to change the subject, I ask, "How are the puppies? I'd love to see them, is Alice at home?"

"No, she 'as gone to ze wholesaler's wiz Rose to get more supplies for ze baking."

"Good, let's go back to yours for lunch. We can do our research there, and I can see the puppies. Can we go and get Shadow? He needs to meet them, too; he is their father." Xavier rolls his eyes but obliges, and parks outside the Chateau. After collecting Shadow, we walk across to the farmhouse. "Where has the sun gone? It was brilliant blue skies when we left this morning."

"Yes, Mama said we would 'ave some rain today; ze crops need it," Xavier replies as he gently takes hold of my hand and continues walking. I tense momentarily, then force myself to relax. It feels comfortable, but is it right?

Alice is in the garden bringing in her laundry when we arrive at the farmhouse, and I shake my hand free from Xavier's with no doubt a look of surprise on my face. She asks with a knowing look, "Hello, where have you been?"

"What are you doing 'ere?" Xavier asks in surprise.

"I happen to live here," Alice replies, laughing.

"We've brought Shadow to meet the puppies," I say, trying to change the subject. Shadow scurries about in the backyard in his usual curious manner then rushes inside, stopping dead as he sees the tatty cardboard box containing three sleepy puppies. He looks back at Xavier with questioning eyes and waits for his command, then approaches it, sniffing around the perimeter. Patch is the first to wake with a yawn and a stretch, which disturbs Pepper, who then does the same. Both puppies spot Shadow, avert their gaze and freeze. "What's wrong with them?" I ask.

"Nozing. They 'ave learned ze lesson and are being submissive." Next, Freckles wakes up and stares at his father. He makes a little yapping noise then struggles over his brothers and approaches Shadow. I hold my breath, expecting an altercation, but Shadow only sniffs at the puppy. Beau is on his bed in the corner and opens his eyes and sits up. I look over to Xavier, who is watching with interest. Will Beau join in and attack poor Freckles?

"What should we do?" I ask anxiously.

"Nozing. Zey 'ave to sort out ze 'ierarchy for zemselves." Beau stands and walks across slowly to the box. Shadow turns and faces the big dog. His hackles begin to rise, and he growls.

"Xavier, do something, they are going to fight!" I shout.

"I 'ave never seen Shadow confront Beau. 'E 'as always been submissive; like 'e should be. Beau is ze pack leader," Xavier replies, not taking his eyes off the situation. "Stand out of ze way. Do not try to interfere. You might get injured." He adds, "Mama, take Laura into ze garden."

"No way, you can't let them fight. I will not let you! Shadow will lose; Beau is far bigger and stronger." The two dogs continue their standoff for what feels like an eternity. Eventually, Beau looks over to Xavier then sits down, quickly followed by Shadow, who lays on his side. "Shadow has won!" I exclaim.

"No, Beau has chosen not to fight; it's not in ze pack interest. Shadow 'as recognised zis and submitted. But what worries me more is ze little puppy, 'e doesn't seem to learn very quickly," Xavier says while scratching his big dog on the head.

"It's early days. Now, what about lunch?" Alice says, looking at me with a warm smile.

7

I walk back to the Chateau with Shadow as the rain begins to fall. "It's just a shower, it will soon pass," I say to him as he scampers on ahead of me. Once inside, I make myself comfortable in the small sitting room and search for more information about the numerous tests the hospital offers. Soon, my eyelids begin to droop, and I put my tablet down. Shadow is asleep at my feet. Exhausted, I rest my eyes and sit back into the plush cushions and drift off.

I'm back in the city hospital, in a small white room with a big glass window. Someone's crying, "Shut up, I'm tired. Please let me sleep!" I moan.

"Come on, Mummy, your babies need feeding," says a woman with an abrupt voice. "Here," she hands me a tiny baby swaddled in a blanket. I take it from her

and look down into the crumpled face of a new-born with piercing blue eyes and masses of ginger hair.

"This isn't my baby!" I cry, trying to hand it back to her.

"Yes, it is; and so is this one," she says, handing me another with dark eyes and brown curly hair. I look up to see Enzo and Xavier fighting on the other side of the glass partition.

"No… No! Stop it..."

"Laura, wake up. Laura…"

"What? Where am I?" I say, sitting up, and gradually coming to my senses. "Xavier, what time is it? Why are you wet?"

"I've been trying to ring you. Zere is ze big storm. We need to 'elp zem at ze campsite. Come on, put your coat and wellies on," Xavier says, pulling me off the sofa.

We step outside into torrential rain, which is blowing sideways in the gusting wind. Climbing into the truck and looking out at the molten lead clouds, I ask, "When did this start?"

"Not long after you left, but it started getting worse about twenty minutes ago. I 'ave opened ze sluice gate on ze pond," Xavier replies, driving at speed across the gravel towards the campsite. As we turn the corner, it looks like we have arrived in a war zone. Men are chasing after chairs and other items being blown by the wind while several tents and their contents splay across the site in soggy piles. The caravans and motorhomes are still standing but swaying a little, their occupants watching out of their windows like prisoners. We jump out of the truck and run across to help the three men trying to retrieve their possessions; wading ankle-deep through a rushing torrent that is running off the far bank and into the field.

"Where are your families? Is anyone hurt?" I shout, having difficulty to make myself heard above the noise of destruction. One of the men points to the small shower block.

"You go and check on ze families, I will 'elp 'ere," Xavier shouts back.

I'm now facing into the wind, and it's a frantic struggle to reach the building with the driving rain stinging my face. I lean forward and try to keep my head down as I gradually make slow progress and eventually reach the refuge. Once inside, the door slams shut behind me with a resounding bang. I look up to see five women huddled together with three children; some of them crying, while two men stand watching the carnage through the small window. As all eyes turn towards me, I ask, "Is anyone injured?"

"No, not in here, but I did see a man over there take a direct hit from a flying chair," one of the men says. I look out of the window to see Xavier and the three men retrieving some of the items and placing them in a pile behind a stone wall.

"Our tent is broken. What are we going to do?" A young girl who is cuddling a bedraggled black Labrador, with her wet hair plastered to her face wails. Her mother places her arms around the child and looks over to me.

"Don't worry, we'll sort something out," I say, wondering the same thing. Right now, I don't know whether to laugh or cry; it looks like a scene from an old comedy film that I watched with my gran, only this time it's not so funny. I kneel beside the young girl and say, "We're safe in here, and as soon as the wind dies down, we'll all go to my house to get dry and have some hot chocolate and cookies."

"But where will we sleep?"

Mm, good question. The tents and equipment look beyond repair. "Oh, I'm sure we can find somewhere, don't worry," I repeat while trying to formulate a plan. Loss of tents and equipment wasn't on the business plan that I submitted to the planning office. I don't think

I'm liable for their loss, but I'd better check my insurance policy.

Xavier and the three men make their way over and struggle inside with some personal belongings. "Teddy! He's soggy!" A little boy called Jules cries.

"'E'll dry," Xavier says, handing him back to Jules, who manages a thin smile.

"Are any of you injured?" I ask as the men stand dejectedly in the room, with puddles forming at their feet. I can see one of them has a trickle of blood running down by his ear. Stepping forward, I ask if I can check his head for cuts.

"It doesn't hurt," he replies, then reminds me that he's called Frank. He bends down, and I can see a small cut between his ear and his eye.

"I'll put a small dressing on that when we get out of here. Have you got a headache or blurred vision?" Frank assures me that he's okay, so we stand and watch out of the window as the storm does its worst for another twenty minutes. Raindrops slam on the roof and meld with their neighbours to form a waterfall that blurs the view out of the window. Then, the lights go out.

"Mummy, Mummy, I don't like it. Make it stop!" Zoe, the little girl, cries.

"Don't worry, it can't last much longer, the cables must have come loose. Xavier will fix them when the storm's over," I say, trying to sound as reassuring as possible. I check my phone and see a message from Alice.

Is anyone hurt? The school are keeping the children in until the storm has passed. Can I do anything?

Gosh, I hadn't thought about Gus. At least he will be safe and dry.

We're all okay. When the storm dies down, we're going to need towels, blankets, hot drinks and snacks. Don't come over until it stops.

"Will the animals be okay?" I ask.

"Yes, zey will shelter in ze stables, don't worry about zem," Xavier replies.

Much to everyone's relief, the howling gale and lashing rain gradually slows, and the sky lightens a shade. "Okay, can everyone make it to the Chateau?" I ask. Everyone nods and the children cheer, and we all exit the little shower block with our heads down, walking like a troop of exhausted soldiers returning from war. Alice has already arrived and distributes warm towels and hot drinks to the weary group, and sweet treats to the children, who appear to have made a remarkable recovery. Xavier gets a call asking him to help ferry the children home from school in his truck, as some of the roads are impassable to smaller cars, and the busses aren't running. "Okay, so now I've got three couples and two families to accommodate," I say to Alice as she puts more wet clothes in the tumble driers.

"Not a problem," she replies.

"I suppose they could have the bedrooms, but it will be a lot of hard work changing all of the bedding again, and I don't think they'll want to pay…"

Alice interrupts with her solution. "I've already agreed with Monsieur le Maire; we can borrow the camp beds and sleeping bags that the scouts use, and they can camp in the downstairs rooms tonight. We can manage a simple supper tonight and breakfast for them in the morning. Then they can make alternative arrangements."

"Do you think they'll find that acceptable?" I ask as the idea sinks in.

"Well, they were camping anyway, so camping inside a Chateau is a bonus; don't you think?"

Xavier arrives back with Gus and the borrowed equipment, and after supper, the now merry troop, having shared several bottles of wine, set up camp. The family with two children and the dog take the drawing-room, the family with only one child take the small sitting room, and the three couples set up camp in the dining room, breakfast room, and library. What could possibly go wrong?

8

Alice helps to tidy up the kitchen then leaves with Gus, while Xavier checks on the animals. Exhausted, I make my way upstairs with Shadow and have a quick shower. I'm about to climb into bed when I hear footsteps on the landing. Perhaps one of the campers has got lost? I pop my head out to find Xavier about to enter one of the back bedrooms. "I didn't want to disturb you, sorry," he says.

"Is everything okay?"

"I'm not 'appy leaving you alone wiz zese people, we need to put a lock on your bedroom door," he says, closing the distance between us.

"Don't worry. I'll be fine. Sleep well, and, thank you for your help today," I say trying to hide my body, clad only in a cotton nightdress.

"Zis is my job, and you are 'aving my child, so yes, I want to 'elp. I don't like you doing ze 'ard work. Now, get some rest; I will make ze breakfasts."

I close the door and climb into bed. Xavier does have a point. I'm sharing my home with strangers. It never occurred to me before. I've sold most of the items of value to pay for the renovation, but I do still have a few lovely pieces left in my possession, and the war memorabilia, which is quite collectable. Should I have some cameras in the public rooms? Something to think about perhaps.

I wake to the sound of piano music, and a barking dog. Either one of my guests is a musician, or Aunt Mary has decided to join us; I fancy it's the latter. I grab my robe and meet Xavier on the landing again. "You know who?" I say with raised eyebrows.

Following me down the stairs, he replies, "Yes, probably. 'Ow are you going to explain zis?"

"I have no idea."

We tiptoe across the hall to see Jules sat on the piano stool, and the black Labrador sat at his side, barking and howling along to the music. Oh dear! Jules's parents look on in amazement from their camp beds, shining a torch towards the noise. Jules's mother, fighting to get out of her sleeping bag, asks, "What's happening?"

The music stops as we enter the room. I peer around me in the gloom, but I can't see Aunt Mary. "I'm so sorry," Xavier says.
"Sometimes Laura sleepwalks, she must 'ave come down and started playing ze piano." He takes me by the arm and pretends to lead me out of the room.

"No! No, that's not what happened. An old lady came and played the music; it wasn't Laura," Jules insists.

"Stop telling stories Jules, and don't shout; you'll wake your sister," his mother says as poor Jules is quickly ushered back to bed. I apologise for waking them and walk with Xavier back into the hall. I somehow manage to make it to the top of the stairs before collapsing in a fit of giggles.

"It was ze first zing zat came into my 'ead," Xavier says, trying to keep a straight face.

"First of all, you blame me for sleepwalking. Then you get an innocent child into trouble for telling lies; I didn't think you had it in you," I poke him in his chest.

"Sometimes you 'ave to be creative; if you 'ad told zem ze truth zey would 'ave ran away screaming, or not believe you. Zis way it's no big deal," he says, taking hold of my finger and placing it between his teeth and applying gentle pressure. I look into his face like a rabbit in the headlights, unsure of what to do next. He releases my finger and gently takes hold of my hand, placing a soft kiss on the back of it, he then continues, "Come on, try and get some rest; it's been a strange day."

"You're not wrong!" I say, rolling my eyes, and leave him standing in the corridor, watching me as I go back to my room. I snuggle into bed feeling better, glad of his presence and have no trouble getting back to sleep.

The morning sunshine wakes me as it lands on my bed and warms my face. I climb out and stretch, then pull back the curtains to reveal azure blue skies. The grass has already lost its yellow tinge. The storm, as destructive as it was, has somehow rejuvenated the earth. I also feel different; invigorated, and ready to move on. I can hear chatter and laughter and smell coffee and chocolate. Xavier has undoubtedly made breakfast for our guests, and I, too, am famished. It's 9.20 am, when did I last sleep this late? All eyes turn to me as I enter the breakfast room.

"So, this is our mystery pianist," Frank says.

"No, Daddy, it wasn't her. It was an old lady in a funny dress!" Jules says in a whiney voice.

"You must have been dreaming, son," Frank says, ruffling the blond hair on the little boy's head.

"Yes, sorry about that. I hope I didn't disturb you," I say.

"'As everyone 'ad enough breakfast?" Xavier asks, quickly changing the subject.

"Yes, thank you; and, thank you for your hospitality. We need to get back to the campsite to see what can be salvaged and decide what to do."

"Ze scouts 'ave very kindly offered to lend you zeir tents and equipment for a few days, until you can get replacement items," Xavier says while handing me a cup of weak black tea. The campers hold a short meeting. Then the men go back to the campsite to salvage what they can, while the women pack up the camp beds and gather their belongings and follow them with their children. Once they've gone, Xavier asks, "'Ow are you feeling?"

"Much better, thank you," I say, tucking into a bacon and cheese baguette, smothered with tomato ketchup.

Xavier looks at me with a confused expression, "You don't like tomato sauce."

I smile back at him and reply, "Well, I do now." He steps closer and wipes a blob of the red sauce off the end of my nose, then plants a tender kiss in its place. I freeze momentarily and look into his alluring eyes, then reciprocate the gesture.

"Oh... Good morning. Erm... What can I do to help?" Alice asks, placing a basket of fresh bread on the kitchen counter, having witnessed our brief display of affection.

"Mama… 'as Gus got off to school all right?"
Alice nods and smiles back at her son with a
knowing look. "I'm going to ze campsite to
check on ze damage and see if I can restore
power to ze shower block. Can you 'elp Laura
to clean up 'ere?"

"Of course."

Xavier departs and leaves me alone with Alice.
Feeling more than a little awkward, I turn on
the small flat-screen TV mounted on the wall
and put the news on as we begin to clear away
the breakfast dishes. "I wonder if they will
mention the storm?" I ask, attempting to
break the silence.

"Probably not. It might be on the local news,
but the station doesn't usually report storms
here unless there's been loss of life. We get
several bad ones every year since we're
between the mountains and the coast. It will
make it into the local paper, but not until
tomorrow's edition. Have you checked the
internet?"

I locate my tablet but can't find much, just a few images on social media of the storm and flooded roads. A man further up the valley had a tree land on his house and suffered minor injuries. I immediately think of Henri, the goat farmer. I hope he's okay. I try ringing his landline, but it gives an odd tone, so I know the line must be down. I know he lives alone. Poor Henri. I remember him telling me he has a son. Surely, he'll check on his father. We move on to the drawing-room, and I tell Alice about Aunt Mary's appearance. "I don't know what to do about it. I can't have her scaring the guests away. It's surreal; if someone else had told me that they had a haunted house, I wouldn't have believed them. You've got to witness it with your own eyes. Have you ever seen her?"

"No, I haven't, but Gus tells me he has. Now, can you help me to move this sofa back against the wall?" She asks, obviously struggling with the large piece of furniture.

I instinctively walk over to help then remember Sweet Pea. Probably not a good idea. "Let's leave that for Xavier. I wonder how he's getting on?" I say, turning my back to her while collecting up the spare pillows scattered on the floor. I don't have long to wait for an answer to my question when a text arrives from him.

Going down to ze village to get ze tents from ze Scout Hut. Back for lunch.

9

"Hello, have they got sorted?" I ask when Xavier returns.

"Yes, and ze power is back on at ze shower block — just a loose wire — but ze phone lines are down in ze valley. It's not unusual,"

Xavier says, sitting at the table and stuffing his mouth with a pie.

"Yes, I've tried ringing Henri. I do hope he's okay…"

"Don't worry about 'im, 'e's used to ze storms…"

"I know, but he's getting old. He won't be able to manage for much longer."

"Xavier, please can you put the sofa back in the drawing-room? Laura thinks it's too big a job for us," Alice says, looking over to me while spreading Pâté on her bread.

"And, Laura is right—"

Alice interrupts her son and asks, "Is there something that you're not telling me? You have both been acting out of character. Is Laura ill?"

Xavier looks first at his mother then over to me, seemingly at a loss for words. I put my knife and fork down and look back into Alice's concerned face. I take a deep breath and say, "No, Alice, I'm not ill. I'm eleven and a half weeks pregnant. I wasn't going to tell anyone until twelve weeks, but…"

Alice jumps out of her seat, sloshing water out of the full glasses as she knocks the table, and is at my side before I have time to think. She pulls me out of my chair and wraps her motherly arms around me. "Why didn't you tell me… Enzo… does he know? I thought you two had split up…"

"Sit down mozer, and give Laura some space…"

Alice lets me go, and I sit back down in my chair. She takes a step back, her eyes not leaving my face. "Yes, Enzo and I have split up… and, it's not his baby," I say quietly while looking at my plate in front of me.

She then looks over to her son in confusion. His face is lit up with pure joy. She stammers, "What… who?"

"It's my baby, Mama; mine and Laura's."

Alice makes it back to her chair and drops down onto its cushioned seat, looking flabbergasted. Turning her head, first to look at Xavier, then back to me, she opens and closes her mouth silently. At last, she says, "I realised that you two were getting closer to each other, but pregnant! Eleven weeks…"

"I'm sorry, Alice, it wasn't planned, and it's my fault; I'd had too much to drink and, well — too much information. Please don't tell anyone."

"What about Gus?" She asks, now looking over to her son.

"We were going to tell you both togezer, next week; I'm not sure 'ow 'e will feel about ze situation."

"Sapristi! I never imagined that you would bless me with any more grandchildren," she says to her son, then asks me, "When are you due?"

"Not until early December; its ages away yet."

"But time goes so quickly, what are you going to do? Which room will you use as the nursery? Are you two getting married?" Alice asks, looking between the two of us. "Have you chosen a name?"

"Mozer, stop! Laura is only just beginning to come to terms wiz ze idea. We 'aven't made any decisions about anyzing yet. It's very early days; please stop getting carried away." Alice sits still with a wondering expression on her face, watching her son, while Xavier continues to pile food on his plate. I look at the mother and son sat side by side and can't help but notice the similarities and differences between them. Alice is short and rotund, while Xavier is tall and muscular. Alice now has grey hair with hazel eyes, whereas Xavier is very dark; Gus undoubtedly favours his father's looks.

"Who does Xavier take after?" I ask, looking over to Alice.

"Oh, he is just like his father. I'll find some photo's out for you; Gus looks like him too.

What about you? Do you look like either of your parents?"

"Mozer, that's insensitive, you know Laura lost her parents when she was a child," Xavier chastises.

"It's okay. I have a few photos' somewhere of my parents and my gran. I ought to display them; I think I'm just a mix of them both. I wish I still had at least one of them left, or a sibling," I say as I feel the sting of tears and I close my eyes. Tears start to fall onto my lap, and I realise I'm crying. I grab my napkin, and dab my eyes, "I'm sorry, I'm so emotional at the moment; I go from euphoria to melancholy in a matter of minutes."

Xavier stands and approaches me, kneels at my side and places a protective arm around my shoulder.

"It's quite normal. It's only your hormones. I'm sorry, I didn't think," Alice adds, offering her hand across the table. "Let me know when you decide to tell Gus. I'll cook a family dinner."

"How are the puppies?" I ask, changing the subject. Alice smiles, fondly, and goes on to tell me about their antics. Patch and Pepper are learning fast, but poor Freckles is somewhat slower.

"I don't zink 'e will make ze truffle dog, but ze ozer two are perfect," Xavier adds.

"Poor Freckles, what will you do with him?"

Xavier shrugs.

"Laura, what else can I do for you while I'm here?" Alice asks, giving Xavier a strange look.

"Erm, I think everything is fine now, thank you. I've got some paperwork to catch up with, and some enquiries to reply to; nothing too strenuous."

"Good," Xavier says, "I picked up a lock while I was out. I'm going to fit it to your bedroom door, zen I will go and inspect ze rest of ze estate for storm damage."

An hour later, and I'm once again alone. I wander through the Chateau, looking for possibilities for a nursery. Of course, Sweet Pea will be in my room for the first year, but then what? I make my way up through the secret staircase into the attic; it has potential. Xavier mentioned turning it into a flat. It would need a better staircase constructing, but it's a possibility. There's no way I can afford to do it any time soon, though I have some money put aside for emergencies. However, I've no intention of dipping into that — a project for the future. Perhaps Sweet Pea will have to stay in my room for a few years. I could have a partition wall put up. Yes, it's big enough. There, problem solved. Now, back to work.

The company that is running the vintage rally want to come out and have a look around the estate to discuss their requirements sometime next week. They also want to stay the night, and they're English too; that sounds interesting. I reply to the rest of my emails and find one from Jenny.

Hey, how are things? I've been worried about you. You didn't seem like yourself last time we spoke. Jacques came over for a holiday and then I went straight onto a run of night shifts. Can we Skype tomorrow? xx

I'd almost forgotten about Jenny, so much has gone on recently. Should I tell her about Sweet Pea? I've practically reached twelve weeks now. Mm, I'll see how it goes.

Yes, I'm okay, busy as usual. We had a massive storm yesterday; more like a monsoon. Skype tomorrow at 7 pm. Xx

I sit back and go over the lunchtime conversation. Poor Alice; she wasn't expecting that, though she seemed thrilled with the news. It's been a big shock for all of us. I hope Gus takes it as well as Alice did. And poor Freckles, will he make the grade? Hmm, Alice quickly changed the subject and gave

Xavier a strange look when I asked what they were going to do with him. That probably only means one thing. What were his words when we found Shadow emaciated and in a poor state of health? *'It needs putting out of ze misery.'* Is that what he intends to do with Freckles? Surely not! I won't let him. I send him a text.

Xavier. Don't you dare do anything to poor Freckles!

I take Shadow and hurry over to the farmhouse, to find no one at home. The three puppies are cuddled together in what remains of the now shredded box. They open their eyes, yawn and roll over onto their short legs. They all look the same, which one is Freckles? Patch still has a faint black smudge on his head from the marker pen, but Pepper and Freckles look alike. Two of the puppies freeze when they notice Shadow, but the third one carries on and bumbles his way towards him. Shadow wags his tail and sits down as the puppy reaches him and begins to gnaw Shadow's back leg. Shadow lets out a yip then bats the puppy on its head, knocking him over. "You must be Freckles," I say, about to pick the little dog up.

"Leave 'im. I want to see what Shadow does."

"Xavier, how long have you been here?"

"Long enough," he replies, this feels like a case of déjà vu!

"What were you going to do with him, Xavier?"

He walks over and squats beside me, looking first at Freckles and then back at me. "'Onestly," he says, "I don't know. What do you suggest?"

"Well, I won't let you put "im out of ze misery'," I say, trying to imitate his thick accent.

He laughs and sits on the floor, letting out a massive sigh, then pauses and takes my hand before saying, "Yes, zere was a time, not so long ago, when zat is exactly what I would 'ave done. But I 'ave changed. You 'ave changed me."

He pauses then closes the distance between us, so our lips are almost touching, then he stills. *Kiss me, why don't you?* My insides are screaming, but he doesn't move. I can no longer stand the tension. I shut my eyes and close the gap, so our lips are touching. I go still. It's like a battle of wills. Who will give in first? Me. I crumble and start to kiss him, gently at first but gradually with increasing passion. Our bodies meet, and it feels like electricity is pulsing between us. When we eventually stop for breath, I realise we're both laid on the kitchen floor in a tangle, with Shadow and Freckles climbing all over us. Xavier bursts out laughing just as Alice appears through the door. She takes one look at us, starts laughing and turns around and leaves again.

10

Xavier helps me up, and we sit at the table watching Shadow and Freckles frolicking about together on the tiled floor. Patch and Pepper take an interest for a short while then doze off together in a corner. "Shadow is good with Freckles, perhaps a few days wiz 'im at ze Chateau would 'elp wiz 'is education."

"Won't he miss the other two?" I ask.

"I don't zink so. Zey often leave 'im out. 'Ave you ever trained a puppy before?"

"No, but it can't be that difficult. When are we going to get the puppies vaccinated? Sara said that they'd already had their first jab."

"I don't bozer wiz zat, too expensive."

"Well, I want them to be vaccinated. I'll call the vet. Damn! I don't want to run into Enzo."

Xavier puts his hand on my knee and replies, "Okay, I will take zem; you ring and tell me when ze appointment is, yes?"

An hour later, I'm back at the Chateau with Shadow and Freckles, and a long list of instructions on how to train him, with no puppy food in sight. Freckles' spends the first hour exploring the kitchen. I leave the back door propped open and encourage him out into the backyard with Shadow and praise them both for doing a wee. Shadow thinks it's fantastic to get a small treat every time he shows Freckles what to do. Positive reinforcement, that's what it's called. Allegedly, it works for children too. Good practice for me then.

After feeding them (Freckles gets his ration of the diced game while Shadow gets his usual biscuits, mixed with a small amount of the chopped game) I then confine them to the kitchen as instructed and bid them goodnight, leaving an old towel near the back door for Freckles, in case he needs a wee in the night. Shadow looks at me with his 'not too impressed' expression as I shut the door on the pair. I drift off to sleep, thinking about today's events.

I'm in the kitchen at the farmhouse kissing Xavier. When I pull back for much-needed air, I find myself looking into a pair of blue eyes and a ginger beard. "No! ... no... where's Xavier..." I'm brought back to reality by a noise startling me awake. What's that? Then I hear it again, a quiet whimpering. Freckles. Oh dear, the poor mite, he's bound to wonder what's happening. First, he was removed from his mother and dumped at the farmhouse with scary Beau, then moved here all within a week. It must be so unsettling for him, but he's got to learn.

I turn over and try to go back to sleep, but it's not happening, the whimpering gets louder and then Shadow joins in the melee. I put a pillow over my head and try to ride it out, but it continues on and on. Xavier said this might happen and that I was not to cave in. An hour later, and I can stand it no longer. I enter the kitchen to find both dogs sat at the back of the door. Shadow dashes past me and runs upstairs, no doubt heading straight for his bed in my room, and Freckles wags his stumpy tail and urinates on the spot. I lift him and place him on the still dry towel by the back door, where he stands, looking confused.

Now, what am I going to do? Xavier was right, as he so often is. It's not that easy, and I need to sleep. I carry Freckles up to my bedroom and put him in bed with Shadow, which doesn't go down too well. Shadow puts his long snout under the little dog's belly and flicks him out on to the floor. Okay, Shadow is allegedly not prepared to share. I grab the first thing I find, which is a large bath towel and shape it into a small nest, plonking the hapless puppy into the middle, so much for not caving in!

The whimpering starts again as soon as the sun rises. Great, it's just turned 7.00 am. I turn over and try to block it out, but poor Freckles persists, then I can feel him tugging on the bedclothes. No rest for me, then! Shadow lifts his head, looks at me and goes back to sleep, "It's your baby you know, you should be looking after him," I say, but Shadow continues to ignore me. "Okay Freckles, let's go out for a wee, then you can have breakfast."

Shadow appears as I serve breakfast to Freckles. What did Xavier say to me in the farmyard when I first arrived? "You 'ave to be ze boss." Yes, I can see that now. These two have already got me wrapped around their little paws! I can do this. I have to do this. Yawning, I look at my favourite search engine for advice: Leave a radio on so they think someone is there. That might well work with Freckles, but I think Shadow is the problem. He's become used to sleeping in my room. He could be jealous when Sweet Pea arrives. Yes, it would be an excellent time to get him trained to sleep downstairs. I'm going to have to be stronger tonight. I leave both dogs in the kitchen while I sit at the table doing my monthly accounts. The takings are steadily rising. I need to ring the vets, and there's no time like the present, "Hello, please can I bring three puppies for their second vaccinations?"

"Certainly, do you have a preference in which veterinarian you see?"

"Erm, anyone, except Enzo, please," I say, feeling a little awkward.

"That's unusual, most of our English clients request to see him," the receptionist says. "He's leaving at the end of the month anyway. I can fit you in tomorrow lunchtime, at noon, with Simone." Oh, my God, he's leaving in two weeks! Was he going to tell me or skulk off home without saying goodbye? "Hello, it appears to be a bad line, are you still there?"

"Sorry, yes. Yes, tomorrow lunchtime is good, see you then," I say and hang up. Oh, I didn't even give the receptionist my name, I don't suppose it matters. I've made the appointment now. I'd better inform Xavier.

Noon tomorrow at the vets, can you manage?

The puppies are going to be a handful, he hasn't even got collars and leads for them. I think I'll pop down to the village to get some. A half-hour later, I arrive back with a new bed for Freckles and three small collars and leads. I immediately put one around Freckles neck. The little dog spends the next hour trying to remove it. What a good idea! I take it back off and leave him to nap for a while. I'll put it back on at bedtime. It will keep him occupied and take his mind off his separation anxiety. With no reply from Xavier, I give him a call.

"Sorry, I was in ze vineyard, tidying up after ze storm."

"Oh dear, are the vines okay?"

"Yes, zankfully. Ze flower buds aren't open yet, anozer two weeks. I saw your text about ze vet. 'Ow did you get on last night?"

"Erm, could have been better."

"I zought zat you would 'ave a bad night. I will come and get 'im—"

"No, don't," I interrupt, "let's give him another try; he's only a baby. I've got some collars for the other two."

"Good, I'll call in and get zem. See you soon, Laura."

I'm making an omelette when he arrives. "Mm, zat smells good," he says, looking over my shoulder.

"Would you like one?"

"Yes. I would very much like to stay wiz you for dinner, but I ought to go back and spend some time wiz Gus. I don't want him to feel jealous of you or ze baby. Sorry."

"Don't be sorry, you're his father, and you have to do what is best for him. I understand. When do you think we should tell him?"

"Sunday lunchtime. Mama is cooking."

"Poor Alice, she's always cooking. What has she said about the… err… situation?"

"She's said very little, but 'asn't stopped smiling. I know she's excited, and, she loves cooking."

Xavier leaves soon after and I eat my omelette alone. After supper, I turn on my computer for my Skype session with Jenny. Her happy face fills my screen.

"Laura, you look much better. How's the situation with you-know-who?"

"I presume you mean Xavier. It's improving, I think."

"Was it a one-off, or are you two still at it?" She asks, with her green eyes twinkling as she winks.

"No, we're not! It's complicated."

"How so?"

In an attempt to change the subject, I ask, "Did you have a good time with Jacques? What did he think to the North of England? I hope it wasn't too wet or cold."

"I thought we were discussing your love life, not mine. However, it went well. He loved the nightlife in the city; I think he'll be back." She smiles. "Now, on to you. Have you put a bit of weight on? Your face looks fuller; it suits you."

I puff out my cheeks, trying to make light of her comment, though people are bound to start noticing soon. Some of my trousers are getting somewhat tight.

I sigh, wondering what to say next when she blurts out, "Don't tell me – you're pregnant!"

Again, I don't speak as I look down at my hand, which is hugging my tummy, so she continues, "You are, aren't you? You're having his child!"

I lift my eyes back up to see her expression has changed to a concerned look. "Yes," I say quietly. "How did you know?"

"Oh, Laura," she says, reaching her hand out towards the screen. "My poor love, I'm going to see if I can get some time off work. I'll ask tomorrow—"

"Jenny," I interject, "you've just had time off with Jacques, surely you've got no holidays left. Seriously, I'm okay now, I've had time to get used to the idea; nearly twelve weeks."

"Does he know?" She asks cautiously.

"God, yes, and Alice, too. They're both thrilled! We're telling Gus on Sunday. I don't know how he'll take it, though."

"Don't worry about Gus. He's even more laid back than his father. Have you had a scan?" Jenny sits and listens patiently, as I give her a week by week history of my pregnancy, including my first trip to the city hospital. "God, you're brave! I don't think I would have kept it. You'll be an amazing mother, and what a fantastic place to bring a child up. I'll book some time off in early December, so I can come over and help. Can I be an honorary aunt?"

"More than that! I'm hoping you'll be a godmother," I say. Jenny beams back at me with a cheesy grin. How I wish she were here.

"Names! What are you going to call it? When will you find out the sex?"

"I've got a scan next week, but I don't want to know what sex it is. And, it's silly I know, but for just now I've called it Sweet Pea." I then have to explain why, while Jenny looks back at me gooey-eyed and tearful. "Do you know what? I think you're worse than me! Now, I have a puppy to train, so I'm going." The last comment extends the conversation further as I put Freckles on the screen.

At last, we say goodbye, and I take Shadow and Freckles into the garden for a pee after feeding them. I must be stronger tonight; the boys are sleeping downstairs! I put the new soft collar on Freckles before settling them both down in their beds and leaving a large bone for Shadow to keep him occupied.

11

I have an early night and take my tablet to bed, allowing myself the weekly indulgence of checking on Sweet Pea's progress. It'll be twelve weeks tomorrow! Sweet Pea is now the size of a plumb. Should I call her Victoria? I might also be able to feel my uterus peeping out over my pubic bone. With that little nugget of information, I can't help but lay down and have a feel. Oh yes! I think I can feel the top of something or is that just wishful thinking? I lay with a grin on my face for some time before continuing my quest for knowledge.

Ooh! I should be doing pelvic floor exercise to strengthen the muscles that will be stretched to their limit as I deliver. Nice! Not something to dwell on just yet. Seriously, I know I should be doing them, I have worked in gynaecology and witnessed the fifty-something women coming in for prolapse surgery. They evidently didn't do pelvic floor exercises when they were pregnant. Okay, my next search is how to perform these pelvic floor exercises.

I find several graphic illustrations detailing the muscles involved and even find some bizarrely shaped weights to purchase that you put inside yourself to train these muscles — a complete workout for your vagina! Should I buy some? I don't think so. I'll do them the old-fashioned way.

I follow the instructions on a YouTube video and get started. There's no time like the present! I catch a glimpse of myself in the large mirror and burst out laughing. The lady demonstrating the exercises doesn't have a face like mine. I look like I'm sucking a lemon while holding my breath. Rule number one, don't forget to breathe, and number two, your facial muscles aren't supposed to be doing the same exercises as your pelvic floor muscles. More practice needed! I sip my chamomile tea and fall asleep.

The sun is beginning to peep over the horizon, painting the sky orange as I hear a familiar noise. Freckles. It's only 6.30 am. I rush down to the kitchen to find him stood on the towel by the back door. "Good boy!" I say as I make a fuss of the little man, which causes him to urinate on the spot. If only I'd thought to open the door first. Shadow opens one eye and looks at me briefly, before closing it again and continuing with his beauty sleep. I put Freckles and the soggy towel in the backyard while I stand and watch him sniff around. He trots back inside, and I follow him, then narrowly miss standing in a puppy-sized poo. Perhaps the kitchen isn't the best place for them. I'm sure the hotel inspector would have something to say about that.

After disinfecting the floor and having breakfast, I set about choosing a new location for his bed. I can't leave him in the hall when I've got guests. The only place is the little sitting-room. It's out of bounds for guests, unless of course, there's a storm that destroys their tents. The carpet in there is old and tatty. When he's finally toilet trained, I can change it. Yes, that's where they'll be sleeping tonight. I move their beds and leave both dogs in there to get used to the idea. I'm heading back to the kitchen with the dogs following when my phone beeps with a text.

I'm on my way to collect ze puppy.

Xavier. Of course, he's taking them to be vaccinated. Less than five minutes later, he arrives.

"Did you 'ave a better night?"

"Yes," I reply while trying to stifle a yawn.

"'Ave a rest, I'll keep 'im for ze afternoon," he says as he takes the wriggling puppy from my arms. "Mama wants to know if you 'ave any requests for lunch tomorrow."

"No, anything, except pheasant, rabbit or goat," I reply, struggling to keep my face straight.

Xavier nods and heads out to the vehicle. He then turns back and says, "Before I forget, ze guests caught in the storm are preparing to leave."

I nod and say, "Thanks. I'll go down and see them off."

With Freckles gone, I check my emails. A Mr Brewer and his colleague Mr Sykes, the people organising the vintage rally, are coming to stay on Tuesday and will be arriving at lunchtime. I'm not sure what these events entail, but it should be fun. I ought to go over and say goodbye to the campers before they leave, so I make my way to the campsite. The builders are coming back next week to dig a drainage ditch along the back of the campground to prevent it from flooding in the future. They insist it should only take a couple of days.

When I return from the campsite, parked outside the Chateau is a small van – I'm not expecting visitors. I wonder who it could be? As I approach, two middle-aged men get out, "Hello, I'm Jake, and this is my assistant Pierre, we're looking for the owner," Jake says.

"Hello Jake, I'm Laura, and that would be me. Are you looking for accommodation?"

"Well, not really. We do want to stay for the night, but we won't require a room," Pierre says.

"Oh, erm, we have a small campsite if you've got a tent…"

"No, no, we don't intend to go to sleep. We want to ask your permission to set up some equipment in various locations inside the Chateau and observe from a distance," Jake says.

"I'm sorry, I'm not sure I understand."

"We're, erm…" Jake says, looking uncomfortable.

"Ghosthunters," Pierre butts in rather loudly.

"Pardon? I don't understand…"

"We read it in a magazine. There was an article with some pictures of you, and it mentioned a ghost playing the piano," Jake continues.

"Well, I'm sorry to inform you that it was only a tale to add a little interest. I've never seen or heard a ghost here. Sorry gentlemen, you're wasting your time. Good day." I walk into the Chateau and close the door behind me. What am I supposed to do now? Ghost hunters indeed! I enter the kitchen in need of a cold drink and the doorbell rings. I look out of the dining room window to see their van hasn't moved. I decide to ask them politely to leave. I open the door to find them both stood looking a little sheepish. "I'd like you both to leave now please."

Jake says in a rather condescending manner, "But, we could find the ghost and help you to get rid of it; you don't want it to scare your guests away, do you?"

"Look, Jake, there are no ghosts here, so please go away," I say sternly and try to close the door, but Pierre is quicker than me and puts his large size nine boot in the way. "Please remove your foot, or I will ring the police."

"I wouldn't do that if I were you, mademoiselle. It wouldn't be good for business, especially if it got out that you were turning away guests that have travelled a very long way," Pierre says menacingly.

Trying not to appear alarmed, I say, "Okay, you go and get your equipment, and I'll show you where to put it."

The two men grin. "That's more like it," Pierre says, and they both turn around to go to their van. I wait until they begin to open the van door then I quickly shut the heavy oak door and lock it with the key, and slide the big bolts across, then hurry to the kitchen to do the same at the back. I can hear the two men banging and shouting as I check and close all downstairs windows.

My first instinct is to call Xavier. I wonder where he is. My heart feels like it's trying to escape from its bony cage as I ring his number, but it goes to voicemail. It's past four, and he should be back from the vets. What should I do now? The two men continue to hammer on the door. I'll ring

Alice. She answers on the third ring, "Hello…"

"Alice, is Xavier there? I need back-up, now."

"He's taken the puppies onto the estate with Beau, what wrong?"

"I've got two unpleasant men banging on the door… I'm getting nervous. He's not answering his phone."

"I know what to do, just a minute…"

I hear Alice take a deep breath then nothing. I begin to panic, "Alice, Alice, are you there?"

"Yes, I've just given the emergency signal on Beau's whistle. He should be here soon." My breath releases on a relieved sigh until she adds, "I'm coming over."

"No, Alice, please don't. I'm not opening the door. It's not safe. Stay on the phone with me. I'm up in the attic now. I've closed the secret door, so if they get in, they probably won't find me." I hear a commotion on the line and Xavier's voice, followed by expletives when

Alice tells him what's going on. "Laura, he's on his way."

I watch from the balcony as Xavier's truck approaches at speed. He opens the door before It's even stopped, and Beau jumps out, ready to protect his family. Xavier follows with his rifle in hand as a rapid conversation quickly deteriorates to shouting and swearing, with Beau poised for action as he snarls and bares his vicious-looking teeth. I can't follow the conversation, but Jake and Pierre, if that's their real names, decide not to chance an encounter with the big dog and scramble back inside their van. They set off in a frenzy of wheelspin, spraying gravel into the air.

"Laura, are you okay?" Xavier shouts frantically. I make my way back downstairs and unlock the front door, take a step towards him then blackness descends.

12

Something cold and wet wakes me up. I'm laid on the sofa in the drawing-room with Alice leaning over me with a damp sponge, "There, how are you feeling now?"

"Erm, groggy. Have they gone?"

"Yes, gone like the wind. They're nasty pieces of work, upsetting you like that."

We both turn to the door as Xavier enters with the village doctor.

"Laura, you're awake!" Xavier says, looking somewhat relieved.

I try to get up, but the doctor advises me to stay where I am. Crouching down beside me, he puts a black leather case on the floor and asks, "Now, can you tell me exactly what happened?" Feeling rather foolish, I recount the story of Jake and Pierre. "That sounds quite an alarming experience," he comments then asks, "have you got any pain anywhere?"

"No, I don't think so, it was probably only a faint. I'm sorry to have troubled you on a Saturday," I say.

"It's no trouble. Now, I'm going to take your blood pressure and have a feel at your tummy; is that okay?" He asks while getting his things out of his case. I nod. He then proceeds to wrap my arm in the pressure cuff. "Hmm, your blood pressure is on the low side, and I've got your blood results from the hospital. You appear to be anaemic, so I'm going to start you on some iron tablets. Other than that, I think all is well. When do you go back to the hospital?"

"She 'as ze scan next week. I will take 'er," Xavier answers before I have a chance to think.

"Good. I want you to rest for a few days. If you have any further symptoms, call me immediately. Perhaps you should report those two men to the police. They might send someone out to keep an eye on the place," he adds.

"Don't worry doctor. I will stay 'ere tonight, so she's not alone. Zank you for coming," Xavier says as he takes a prescription from the doctor and shows him out.

Gus comes out of the kitchen with a glass of water for me. He asks, "Laura, what did the doctor say, what's wrong with you?"

I take the glass from him and look over to Xavier for help. He only shrugs, and helplessly looks over to his mother. Taking the bull by the horns, I say, "Alice, please will you prepare a tray with tea and cake, then we could perhaps have a chat together."

"Strawberry smoothie for me, please," Gus adds, lifting the lid of the piano and settling down to play.

"Laura doesn't need zat noise just now—" Xavier protests.

I interrupt him, saying, "Gus, I'd love to hear you play. What are you practising at the moment?" Gus beams back at me and begins to tell me about his music lessons at school as his hands move over the keyboard. "I wish I could play," I say, settling back into the cushions while listening to him tinkle out a tune.

"I'll teach you," he says above the music. He is such a sweet boy. I hope the news he's about to receive doesn't upset him too much. I'd hate to come between him and his father.

Alice arrives back with the tray and a strawberry smoothie as requested, and Xavier beckons for his son to join us. Gus squeezes in between his father and his Nana on the sofa opposite me and looks over in concern. "What's wrong with Laura?"

Neither of them speaks, so I take a big breath and reply, "Gus, nothing is wrong with me really; I'm expecting a baby."

"Cool. Oh, by the way, Dad, I'm going to football practice after school on Monday, so I'll be late back," he says casually. I look over to Xavier, who looks back at me, a little shocked at Gus's easy acceptance. Come on, Xavier, this is where you need to tell him that it's your baby, and it will be Gus's brother or sister. But the words remain in my head, unspoken, as Gus stands then hesitates before saying seriously, "I hope those nasty men don't come back. Dad, I think you and Beau should stay here with Laura tonight." Gus then picks the now empty tray up and takes it back to the kitchen, shouting, "Nan, what's for tea?"

"Well, that went well – why didn't you tell him?" I say while Xavier and Alice look back at me with a look of bewilderment.

"Erm, well, at least 'e knows you're 'aving ze baby; I'll tell 'im soon," Xavier says.

"Yes, we'll tell him over lunch tomorrow," Alice adds, standing to follow her grandson into the kitchen.

"How are the puppies?" I ask.

"Zey are all okay. I left zem at 'ome when Mama called for Beau wiz ze whistle. 'Ave you still got ze whistle I gave to you?"

"Erm, yes, somewhere," I say attempting to get off the sofa.

"Stay where you are," he motions with his hand. "Tell me, and I'll find it, you need to keep it safe. Zree quick, short sharp blows are ze emergency call for Beau."

"Xavier, I'm okay. I only fainted. I can't spend the next six months laid on this sofa. I have to get on with life." I stand carefully and test my legs. They appear to be working, so I help Xavier hunt for the whistle. It is in the desk drawer in the hall. Xavier tries to drape it around my neck, but I refuse and hang it on a small hook by the front door.

"I 'ave to go to do ze animals. Lock ze doors and don't do too much; I will be back later. I'm leaving Beau 'ere."

Xavier instructs his dog to sit guard in the hall. I find him an old blanket and place it at his side, but he refuses to move from the spot where his master left him. I try and tempt him with some sausage, but nothing works, so I leave him sitting in the hall while I search the kitchen for ingredients to make supper.

"Do you think they'll come back?" I ask later as Xavier clears the dishes away.

"Not if zey know what's good for zem. Beau will 'ave to stay 'ere for a while; I'll take ze puppies."

"What about Freckles? Can't I keep him?"

"You 'ave more zan enough to keep you busy. I don't want 'im keeping you awake at night. You need to rest," he says as he looks over to catch me yawning. "Come on. It's bedtime."

"It's not even dark yet," I whine like a spoilt child, but I know he's right, so I obediently take Shadow upstairs for an early night, leaving Xavier finishing off in the kitchen. My eyes are drooping, and I can't even be bothered to shower as I climb into bed, falling into a deep sleep.

I'm woken sometime later by my tablet informing me that someone has entered the drive. It's dark, and I have no idea what the time is. I glance over to the dressing table where I left the tablet charging but can't be bothered to get out and check. It's nearly always wild boar or an intoxicated guest returning to the campsite. I decide it's probably the latter. I instantly drop back off to sleep, feeling safe. Xavier is here with Beau.

13

A distant noise permeates through my slumber — the sound of something shattering

— glass. Beau barks and vicious snarling follows. Shadow jumps up and joins in, scratching at the door to be let out. I leap out of bed, and the room spins. *It's not the best time to faint, Laura.* I stand for a moment while it subsides, then grab my robe and open the bedroom door to let Shadow out. He runs along the landing to the glass door that exits onto the fire escape at the rear of the building, where I see Xavier stood with his gun aimed into the night. "Who was it? Have they gone?"

"Shhh," he whispers, briefly pointing to the staircase up to the attic. I nod and follow his instructions, shutting the secret door behind me. I make it onto the balcony in time to see a vehicle, possibly a small van, leaving at speed with Beau following on behind. Was it the ghost hunters coming back? The hairs on the back of my neck stand to attention as I feel Xavier's presence behind me. He tenderly places his arms around my middle, "Zey've gone now, are you okay?"

My brain seems incapable of informing my mouth it needs to speak, so I lean my head back onto his solid shoulder and eventually manage, "I am, now." I twist my body around and gaze into his face. Xavier's disturbed features relax as he looks back at me. "Thank you," I add before placing a tentative kiss on his lips. He slowly responds as his stubbly chin makes contact.

"Sorry, I 'aven't shaved," he says, pulling back and rubbing his hand across his face.

"I'm sure it wasn't the first thought you had when the ghost hunters woke you. If it was them?"

"Probably, but I don't zink zey were looking for ghosts; treasure 'unters more like."

"Mm, and I doubt that Pierre and Jake are their real names. We should have some images of them from the cameras on the gate posts. Should we ring the police?"

"I'm not sure. You go back to bed while I fix some board over ze broken glass…"

"I'm not tired now. I'm going down to make some tea," I say, standing on my tiptoes and giving him a quick kiss on his lips. We find Beau stood to attention in a pile of broken glass by the fire escape on the landing. "Oh Beau, are you okay?" I ask, picking my way through the shards, trying to get to him. Xavier pulls me back and calls the dog, who immediately obeys and walks through the debris to his master's side. "Is he okay?"

"Yes, 'e 'as paws of steel," he says with pride, scratching the big dog on his head, before doing a thorough sweep of the Chateau. Xavier then allows me downstairs to make tea while he secures the fire escape door and clears away the mess. "You can't stay 'ere alone," he says, finishing his drink.

"What option do I have, Xavier? It's my home. Anyway, Aunt Mary lived here on her own for many years…"

"Yes, but zat was before people knew about ze place. Now it 'as a website and 'as been in a magazine and ze newspapers. Ze 'ole world knows of its existence and your subsequent wealth. It's attracting criminals as well as clients."

"What am I supposed to do? It's the only way I can afford to stay—"

"Come on, it will be daylight soon; you need to rest," he interrupts, "I will sleep on ze landing wiz Beau." My protests fall on deaf ears as he erects a small camp bed outside my bedroom door and ushers me into bed. I leave my door open and laid in the half-light, listening to the reassuring rhythm of his breathing. I could get used to this.

A kiss on my forehead wakes me. Xavier gradually comes into focus as I open my eyes. He's smiling down at me and carrying a tray in his hands. "What time is it?" I ask groggily, forcing my body to sit up.

"Just after 9 am. 'Ow are you feeling?"

"I'm fine. What time did you get up? You must be exhausted," I say, but he only shakes his head and shows me the grainy images that the cameras captured; the number plate not quite readable. "I think we should ring the police," I say.

"No, not yet. I will make some enquiries…"

"No Xavier. We need to report this. They might keep coming back. What would I have done if I'd been by myself last night?"

Sighing, he sits on the bed beside me and takes my hand, lifting it to his lips, "I am not going to leave you alone 'ere, it's not safe at ze moment."

"You can't stay here indefinitely—"

He interrupts, cocking his head to one side, "Why? Don't you like 'aving me 'ere?"

I snuggle into his side as he puts his arm around my waist. "Yes. Yes, I like having you here, but you have Gus and Alice to consider; it's not fair to them."

He runs his hand through his long hair with a look of frustration on his face, then his expression changes as he has an idea, "You could come and stay at ze farmhouse wiz us."

"It's a lovely idea, Xavier, thank you, but you don't have a spare room for me, and I've got guests here on Tuesday. Life has to continue. We both have commitments." Reluctantly, he stands and takes his phone out of his pocket and rings the Gendarmerie Nationale.

"Zey are sending someone over today but can't give you a specific time. Mama will 'ave to cook Sunday dinner 'ere. I'll ring 'er."

Later, I recount last night's events to Alice and Gus in the kitchen as they prepare Sunday lunch. "You can't stay on your own here," Alice insists, echoing Xavier's earlier words.

"Let's see what the Gendarmerie Nationale have to say before we make any decisions," I say, trying to deflect the conversation, though I know they're both right.

"Why aren't they here yet?" Alice replies with frustration. "Gus, go and look out of the window at the front and see if you can see anything."

"It's not an emergency, Alice. We're all safe and well…"

"You should have rung them in the night; they might have been able to catch them…"

"Nana! They're here!" Gus shouts from the hall.

I look out of the window to see a police car coming down the drive and immediately text Xavier, who is out on the estate. He arrives a little after the two Gendarmerie Nationale officers have introduced themselves and have settled down with coffee and cake. I tell the two officers about my visit yesterday afternoon from Pierre and Jake, the supposed ghost hunters, then Xavier takes over by informing them of last nights attempted break-in.

"It seems you were fortunate that Monsieur Besnard had the presence of mind to stay with you last night. What plans have you got in place for tonight?" The older of the two men asks. His young colleague sends the images from the security cameras to the police station. Xavier continues communicating with them rapidly in French, most of which goes over my head. After reading my statement back to me, the two men leave, informing us that a scene of crime officer will be with us shortly to look for fingerprints and any other possible evidence. Well, that's today taken care of, then.

Alice refuses to let me clear away the dishes, insisting that Gus will help her. When they are out of earshot, I dig Xavier in the ribs and whisper, "I thought you were going to tell Gus that you're the father of this baby."

"I zink we 'ave 'ad enough disturbance today. I'll tell 'im after your scan tomorrow, zen 'e can 'ave a photo of ze baby. Yes?"

"Okay, if that's what you think is best."

"I do. I'm going back out on ze estate to carry on working. Ring if you need me, I'll be back for supper. And, yes, I'm staying over. Not negotiable," he says with a stern expression on his face.

14

"The scene of crime officers couldn't find any fingerprints. The two men were wearing gloves. The number-plates were false too. They don't have any leads to work on," I say to Xavier as we eat supper.

He looks over to me and shrugs. "I expected as much," he answers between mouthfuls of chicken salad sandwiches.

"We need to get the fire escape door repaired…"

"I've rung Gustave who did ze roof and balcony. He's coming over to do it. I don't know what else we can do to improve ze security. Beau will 'ave to stay 'ere…"

"Let's not talk about it anymore. It's a lovely evening. I want to go for a walk before it gets dark…"

"You are not going out alone. We should get Shadow and ze puppies and take zem out onto ze estate; it will be good for zeir training."

As we walk, Beau marches in front of our entourage with his head held high, clearly the pack leader. While Patch and Pepper eagerly follow Shadow around, mimicking his actions as he stops to sniff and explore. Freckles' takes no interest in the other dogs but walks beside me, looking cautiously around. We make our way over to the orchard; the blossom now replaced with miniature fruit. Xavier takes hold of my hand and grasps a small apple between his finger and thumb, then says, "See, ze rain 'as 'elped to swell ze fruit, zere will be plenty in ze autumn."

"Yes, it's not the only thing that's beginning to swell. I can't fasten any of my clothes," I say sorrowfully, taking Xavier's hand and placing it on my slight bump. He turns to me and grins like a young boy.

"Yes, I 'ad noticed. We will get you some new clothes tomorrow in town."

He offers me his lips for a tender kiss, which I return; slowly at first but then with a growing passion. His hands trace the curve of my neck and slide down over my white blouse with its button's barely meeting before he gently cups my swollen breast. I drag in a lungful of air as the overly sensitive nipple responds to his caresses. Looking a little concerned, he asks, "Am I 'urting you?"

I don't answer but push myself into his hard body; feeling his masculinity beneath the thin fabric. A groan escapes his lips as he takes my hand and leads me back to the Chateau, with the pack turning tail and following. Once inside, Xavier locks the door and leans me against the wood panelling in the hall, renewing his passionate embrace. I arch my aching body towards him as his hands begin to explore.

"I need you," he whispers.

"I need you more…"

He gently lifts me off my feet and carries me upstairs before depositing me carefully on my bed. I start to fumble with the buttons which are straining to hold my blouse together. "Let me," he says, taking over the task.

I discard my shirt once the buttons are open, and his fingers follow the contour of my breasts; now overflowing from their lacey prison. Xavier reaches behind me and unclips my bra, giving me instant relief. Our eyes meet, and he licks his lips before leaning over me; his tongue now tracing the same path his fingers have just left. We both groan when his hot mouth envelopes the sensitive area.

Drawing back to gauge my reaction, he asks, "Too much?"

"More," I whisper, guiding his head back to my wanting body.

Removing his trousers, he asks, "Are you sure zis is what you want?"

"I'm sure…" I don't manage to finish my sentence before he climbs onto the bed.

"Wake up sleepyhead," says a voice in the distance. I open my eyes to find Xavier once again delivering breakfast in bed. I could get used to this. "Are you okay?" He adds, sitting beside me.

I slowly sit up, testing my limbs. "I seem to be still in one piece," I reply, feeling like the cat that got the cream.

"We need to be away in an 'our. I've run you a warm bath."

Saucily, I ask, while gorging on warm croissants with cherry jam, "Are you going to join me?"

Xavier shakes his head and laughs. "If I did, we would never get zere on time."

The roads are busy with the Monday morning commute, but we arrive at the small hospital with a few minutes to spare. My mind returns to my last hospital visit, where I witnessed a young couple securing their new infant into their car. Now I feel happy and settled too. Gone is the foreboding sense of guilt and shame. I feel like a different person. I shall be forever grateful to the psychiatrist who persuaded me to take some more time to think things through. I can't even remember his name.

"Ready?" Xavier asks, breaking through my thoughts as we walk into the cramped foyer. I nod and grin, taking his outstretched hand as we find the antenatal department. A little later, Xavier stares intently at the screen as the image of our baby appears before our eyes. He looks over to me, squeezes my hand then concentrates once more on the picture of his child.

"Is it okay?" I ask the technician.

"Everything appears to be as we would expect for twelve weeks," the young woman replies while concentrating on the screen. "How many prints would you like?"

"Four, please," Xavier answers before I get a chance to reply. He waits in a queue to pay for the prints while I rush to find a toilet, having drunk the mandatory quota of water on the way here. I return to see him gazing down at the pictures in his hand, oblivious to my presence.

"May I see?"

He gives two of them to me and places the other two carefully into his shirt pocket. "I'm going to give one to Gus," he adds, patting his chest, then changes the subject, "Shopping next, I zink."

"Erm, food first, then shopping. I'm starving."

"What 'ave you got in mind?"

"I could murder pie and peas right now!" I say.

Xavier looks at me with a frown across his brow, "What is pie and peas, exactly?"

"A local delicacy from back home; spicy pork wrapped in shortcrust pastry swamped with mushy peas. My gran loved it."

Xavier looks back at me, perplexed. "I don't zink we can get zis 'ere, let's go into town and see what we can find." Xavier parks the Yeti in a small back street and leads me to an area I've not previously explored. We enter into a small charcuterie with a red and white stripy awning; it smells fantastic. "If we can't get your pork pie 'ere, zen we can't get it anywhere."

An older gentleman wearing a white apron pops out from behind a door and asks what we would like to purchase. Xavier speaks rapidly in French, describing my pork pie. "Mais oui – tourtiere," the man says, tapping his nose. He then produces a family-sized pie with a thick golden crust.

"Is zis what you want?" Xavier asks.

"Yes, but ours are smaller — big enough for one," I say.

"So, we can share ze tourtiere," Xavier replies, then asks the man to cut it into quarters. My mouth waters as he hands me a thick slice and I can't wait to taste it. I take a bite of the still-warm pie, and the salty juice runs down my arm. All eyes are on me as I savour the moment.

"Magnifique!" I say. "Merci monsieur," I add as I lap up the juice from my hands.

The butcher smiles at my compliment. "You can get ze tin of 'mushy peas' in ze big supermarket; so ze tourists tell me," he adds as he gives Xavier his change.

"'Appy now?" Xavier asks as we make our way back to the main street.

"Very. Save a piece for Alice, then perhaps she can make some. I'm sure our English guests will appreciate them too.

"New clothes," Xavier says, steering me into the familiar department store; Jenny's favourite. Reading the signs, he takes me to the mother and baby area, where I accidentally found myself a few weeks ago. The beautiful swinging crib is still set up, and I can't help but go and touch it. Xavier looks at me and smiles then turns to the maternity wear hanging on racks. "What do you need – besides new bra's, and blouses?" He says, smiling as he remembered last night.

"Everything. It's going to be expensive. I'll only get a couple of outfits. I'll have to wash them more often." I look around, but the choice is limited. I choose a canary yellow sundress, two skirts, a couple of pairs of knee-length trousers and some oversized T-shirts. "This will have to do," I say, getting my purse out.

"I'm paying. After all, it's my fault too," Xavier says, taking the items from me. After paying for the clothes, we head back to the Yeti. Xavier rests his hand on my knee as he drives home, seemingly unable to take the big grin off his face.

15

Turning into the drive, I sense his demeanour abruptly change. "What's wrong?" I ask.

Xavier points down the drive to the familiar Land Rover parked near the front door. "What does 'e want?"

Oh dear. Enzo. "I don't know. I thought he'd gone back home."

"I wish 'e would."

"Xavier, you do not need to be concerned. Our relationship is over."

Slamming the Yeti's door as he gets out, he asks, "Zen why is 'e sniffing around 'ere?" Oh dear, I have a feeling this isn't going to be very pleasant.

"Oh, Xavier, how are you? I was looking for Laura…" Enzo says.

"And now you've found 'er. You 'ave a nerve turning up 'ere."

"I know. I'm sorry. I only want a few minutes with Laura. Then I'll be on my way. Not that it's any of your business," Enzo replies, beginning to sound cold.

"What affects Laura is my business…"

"Enzo, how are you?" I ask as I clamber out of the Yeti with my shopping, trying to interject some decorum.

Xavier looks over to me with a hard stare. "Do you want me to get rid of 'im?"

"No Xavier. Let's all go inside and get a cold drink…"

"Whatever 'e wants to say can be said out 'ere, I'll get ze water," Xavier says, opening the door and taking my bags from me before heading inside.

I gesture for Enzo to sit at the table outside, then sit opposite him. Enzo leans forward and tries to take my hand, but I remove it from the table and lean back.

"Enzo, why are you here?"

He sighs and rubs his hand through his scruffy ginger beard and looks at me then says, "Laura, I'm sorry things ended the way they did with us. It was my fault—"

"Yes, it was," Xavier interrupts, angrily banging three glasses of water down on the table. I'm surprised they didn't shatter.

"That's not helpful, mate," Enzo says.

"I'm not your mate!" Xavier replies, towering over Enzo.

"Xavier, please would you give us a few moments — alone…"

Xavier stares at me before stomping off into the Chateau, instructing Beau to sit at my side.

"Are you two an item?" Enzo asks, pointing towards the door.

"Yes. No. Oh, I don't know…"

"Is it his baby or mine?"

I sigh, then lean forward slightly and say, "It's Xavier's baby."

"Are you sure? If it's mine – I'll support you…"

"No, Enzo, it can't possibly be yours."

"Were you sleeping with him at the same time as me?"

"That's enough, Enzo. I think you should leave now before you make things worse," I say, raising my voice a little. Beau stands and stares at Enzo, giving him a warning growl.

"And that's all the thanks I get for tending to the big guy when he was injured…"

"Yes, 'e is very loyal, but 'e won't attack you unless I give 'im ze command," Xavier says, returning.

"Which you're not going to do," I add, looking back at him sternly.

"Laura, I'm going home tomorrow. I only wanted the chance to say goodbye. I hoped to part on good terms."

"Perhaps you should have sent a text in advance to let me know you were coming. It's a bit of a shock to see you, you know," I say, standing up, signalling the end of Enzo's welcome. "Goodbye Enzo, and best wishes; I hope things work out for you," I say, offering him my hand.

He stands and looks over to Xavier. "Take good care of her, mate. You're a lucky bloke," he says then strides over to his vehicle and drives away.

I watch him disappear through the gate posts, and heave a sigh of relief then turn to face Xavier. Before I say anything, Xavier says coldly, "I'm going to do ze animals. Lock ze door," and walks away, leaving me standing on the drive with Beau, wondering what I've done wrong.

I stare at his back then shout, "Xavier, what's wrong? Come back so we can talk!" However, he only hesitates a little then continues to walk away. What is wrong with this man? It's supposed to be me that's hormonal and moody, not him. "You are behaving like a spoilt child!" I shout as he turns the corner and disappears from view. What is the matter with him? He'd been so attentive and thoughtful recently. I thought the days of him giving me whiplash were behind us.

By late afternoon there's still no sign of Xavier. Feeling deflated, I take my unopened bags upstairs and clear a space in my wardrobe, reluctantly putting my favourite shorts and tops to one side. Will they fit me next summer? I hope so. After stowing away my purchases, I change into a new, comfy bra and a pair of old yoga pants and, with little enthusiasm, start to perform the exercises from the sheet that the physiotherapist gave me. She also suggested a website that had more activities and information; another day, perhaps.

My eyes can't stop straying over to my bed, where, last night, Xavier and I shared a passionate embrace. Now he's gone off in a jealous huff. Exhausted by today's highs and lows, I curl into a ball and concentrate on the new image of Sweet Pea that I saw this morning. I stand and find the photos in my bag and place one on the pillow and then lay next to it, drifting off into a fitful sleep.

I'm in an airport, and the nasally female voice over the public address system announces, "The flight to Glasgow is now boarding at gate sixteen." I look up from my seat as a nurse snatches the ginger-haired baby from my breast and walks through the gate and onto the plane.

I wake up in the half-light, sweating, with my hair plastered to my face and my heart racing. Beau jumps up onto my bed, ready to pounce on my attacker, but there's no one there. I concentrate on my breathing as I scratch the big dog in his favourite place, trying to reassure him that I'm not in any danger. I look at the clock. "It's 8.40 pm, where is your master?" I ask but get no reply.

Beau follows me downstairs. Xavier's nowhere to be found. Starving once more, I eat another portion of the cold pie, enjoying the savoury tang of the jelly as it melts on my tongue. Gran would have loved this. Alice comes to mind. I need to get the remaining piece to her before I'm tempted to devour it. It's too dark to walk over to the farmhouse alone now, and with a sense of déjà vu, realisation dawns that it's probably prudent to leave Xavier to stew. I'll send her a text instead.

Hi Alice, we picked up a delicious pie called a tourtiere earlier, I've saved a piece for you hoping that you might be able to recreate it. X

I resist the temptation to ask if Xavier's at home.

Laura, how did the scan go? Xavier's here, but he's not very communicative. Is something wrong? X

Oh dear, what do I say now – and no mention of the pie.

All is well with the baby; he has some photo's – I thought he would have shown you one. What about the pie?

At least I know his whereabouts.

Thank goodness, I was beginning to worry. Yes, my mother used to make one every Christmas, I'm sure I'll have the recipe somewhere. What has he done wrong now? I thought his social skills were improving. X

It would have been easier to phone, but knowing Alice's matchmaking tendencies, I don't want to risk her handing the phone to Xavier.

Nothing major. Perhaps you could drop by in the morning, I have two guests booked in and would appreciate some help with food preparation. Sleep well. X

There. Thinking of guests, I'd better clean up a little and do a bit of dusting. Perhaps I should ask Alice to take Beau home with her in the morning; not everyone likes dogs.

16

My alarm wakes me at 7.30 am. I've got a busy day ahead. My guests, Mr Brewer and Mr Sykes, will be arriving for a late lunch. I stand longer than necessary under the hot shower, enjoying the sensation on my aching muscles. As I step out of the cubicle, I hear a noise. "Hello!" I shout nervously — where's Beau? I cautiously poke my head out of my ensuite to find Xavier arriving with a tray of tea and toast. "Oh, it's you," I say, clutching a towel around my dripping body.

He looks at me with regret written all over his face, takes two steps towards me then hesitates before saying, "Erm, I'll leave you to get ready; I'll be in ze kitchen if you need me." He then walks away, with Beau following closely behind. I dress in one of the new skirts and a large T-shirt and stand before the mirror. I don't look pregnant yet, just a little chunkier; not perfect but it will have to do. I'll need to get something smarter for work and weddings; the next one isn't for a few weeks, eBay perhaps? But not today. I've got work to do.

"Good morning," I chirp as I enter the kitchen.

Xavier has his back to me, loading crockery into the dishwasher. He pauses before turning around. "Laura, about yesterday. I'm sorry," he says, looking a little embarrassed.

"Well, you did rather overreact…"

"Yes. I am an idiot, ze red mist descended…"

"Mm, but you can't come over all caveman every time you feel threatened. Not that you have any cause to be worried. As I said, Enzo and I are over, and he's leaving today." Xavier nods his head slightly and runs his hand over his stubbly chin. I continue, "We have clientele arriving today, you need to change and shave if you plan to be here."

He makes short work of the distance between us and takes both of my hands, looking directly into my eyes, "Can we start again? Please."

I look away briefly, then return my eyes to meet his. "Xavier, our relationship seems to have so many stop-starts. It's like a journey on a London bus."

"But I 'ave never been on ze London bus," he says, with the beginnings of a smile on his lips. How can I resist this man with his dry, sarcastic humour and Neanderthal qualities?

"We'll see," I reply, turning away from him, resisting the temptation to cave in this time.

"What do you need me to do today?"

"Everything's under control. Your mum is coming over once Gus has left for school to help with the food side of things. I'm not quite sure what our guests want to do. They said in their email that they want to have a good look around to see where they can park their cars for the lunch halt and organise a driving test of some sort." I wave my hand vaguely as I continue, "It's going to be quite an undertaking; they are estimating one hundred guests for lunch, the most we've ever had to serve. We're going to need help."

"Hmm, when is it exactly?"

"Middle of July. It will be hot and dry…"

"You can't guarantee zat," he says. "You may recall a certain storm last summer which rendered you unconscious," he adds, trying to keep a straight face. "Seriously, one hundred guests for lunch is too much for you; we need to get caterers to 'elp, yes?"

It will reduce the profits, but he's probably right, so I say, "Agreed."

"Good. Now, I'm going out on to ze estate, ring if you want me."

"Okay, I think you should take Beau with you, though. Alice will be here soon, so I'll be fine."

By 11.30 am, we've prepared enough food to feed a small army, and I suggest we stop. Alice agrees eagerly. "You can freeze what isn't needed, you've got more guests booked in at the weekend," Alice says. "Anyway, are you going to tell me what Xavier did to upset you yesterday?"

"Enzo turned up to say goodbye, and it wasn't me that got upset…"

"Oh, I see. Yes, Xavier can get quite possessive. It was tough when Gus's mother left, but he coped remarkably well."

"Alice, you have both done an amazing job of raising Gus. He's a lovely boy, and I will never prevent any of you from being a large part of this baby's life, even if things don't work out

155

between Xavier and me. Has Xavier told Gus yet that he's the baby's father?" Alice shakes her head, looking defeated. I wonder what he's waiting for, but decide not to ask. It's not for me to interfere.

We have an early lunch, sampling the abundance of food that we've just prepared, including Enzo's family recipe for chocolate chip ice-cream made with goat's milk, which has just become my new favourite. Alice leaves when I receive a text from my guests, announcing that according to their sat-nav, they should be arriving in twenty minutes.

The doorbell rings and I count to twenty before answering. "Mr Brewer, Mr Sykes, welcome; do come in," I say, offering the two men my hand.

"Hello, Miss Mackley. I'm Simon Brewer," he shakes my hand, "please call me Simon; lovely to meet you at last."

"Likewise, and please call me Laura."

"I'm Richard, pleased to meet you," his colleague says, shaking my hand too.

"Would you like a hand with your bags?" I ask, remembering my encounter with the hotel inspector. Both men refuse my offer of help, so I show them to their rooms, suggesting they come down for lunch once they've unpacked.

After a light lunch, Simon and Richard are eager to look around the estate, explaining that fifty cars, each containing a driver and navigator, will arrive at approximately one-minute intervals, and a buffet lunch would be the best option so that they can be on their way again as soon as possible. Okay, that sounds easier than I first thought. "What about this test that you mentioned?" I ask.

"Oh, we would like to set up some traffic cones in the farmyard area at the back of your property to test the driving skills of the crews; it's not as complicated as it sounds, and we would take care of the rally side of things. All you have to do is provide lunch," Simon replies as we walk along the proposed route.

"The drive out of the back of the Chateau is quite rough and bumpy; as you can see," I say apologetically, gesturing towards it.

"Oh, don't worry about that; it adds to the drama," Richard comments. "Thank you for your time, do you mind if we take some photographs and measurements of the farmyard so we can plan the test?"

"No, I don't mind at all."

"Then we're going out to do some route checking, so we'll see you at 7 pm for dinner," Simon quickly adds, "if that's okay?"

I nod, and I leave the two men to get on with their task while I head back to the Chateau to contact the caterers that we've used previously. I arrive to find Xavier and Gustave replacing the fire escape door.

"'Ow did it go?" Xavier asks.

"Good," I say and go on to explain what is required, "I'll get on to the caterers, you spend the night with Gus, you need to tell him about the baby."

"I should be 'ere, what if ze ghost 'unters return?"

"I've got Simon and Richard here, and the door will be fixed and alarmed; I'll be fine."

17

What's left of the week passes by in a blur of work and trying to avoid spending time alone with Xavier. I think I love him, but I thought I loved Enzo and look where that got me. No, I need to be sure. Positively sure before I invest any more into this relationship. We will always be friends; no matter what else happens, we can co-parent. I've reached week thirteen, and I'm beginning to feel better. According to the website, I should soon become radiant. Sweet Pea is now the size of a lemon. Perhaps I should call her sweet and sour! Ooh, I should feel an increase in my libido — another good reason not to spend time alone with Xavier! I also need to get myself a fitness regime. Allegedly, it will make labour easier; that's what the physio said to me too.

Running's a bad idea, and I don't have a pool, so I guess it will have to be walking. Pilates is supposed to be excellent exercise. I'll see if I can find a class, Sylvie might know of one. I should be starting to show soon, and I need to buy bigger clothes. Yes, I can tick that off my to-do list. I've ordered some maternity leggings and shorts with flowing blouses online, along with an elegant dress for weddings; that will have to suffice.

I have the Chateau to myself again after a busy weekend for a fiftieth birthday party, with all five guest rooms full. Alice and Xavier were a great help doing most of the cooking and cleaning, leaving me with only the front of house duties. Time to put my feet up, but first, I think I'll walk over to the campsite. The workmen should be here to dig some drainage ditches near the far bank now, to prevent the field flooding again in the next big storm.

When I arrive, Xavier is already on-site, giving out instructions. Everything appears to be under control, so I take myself off for a walk around the estate with Shadow. I'll collect the puppies from the farmhouse and take them with me. Arriving at the farmhouse, I notice Alice is busy making cheese and ice-cream, so I leave her to it, and head for the pond with the puppies. Shadow jumps in, alarming the resident ducks. Patch and Pepper follow their mentor, enjoying a good splash around the edge. Freckles, however, cannot be persuaded to join in and sits obediently at my side, watching his siblings playing. The warm sun caresses my skin, and my eyelids begin to droop. An annoying ringtone wakes me only minutes later, its Xavier.

"Laura, you need to get 'ere now, we 'ave ze big problem."

"What, where?" I ask groggily.

"Ze workmen, digging, now."

"What's the problem?" I ask but realise he's gone. I hurry over, dropping the dogs at the Chateau en-route, to find Xavier and all four workmen crowded around an area near the bank. "What's wrong?" I shout, breathing hard as I approach. Nobody answers, they only look at me with a shocked expression on their weathered faces.

"Bones," Xavier states. "At first I zink zey belong to a sheep or boar zat 'as died, zen we found zees," he says holding out his hand.

"What are they?"

"Brass buttons, and a cross on a chain…"

"You think it's a body?" I ask.

"Oui," one of the other men answers quietly.

"Oh, my God! What should we do? I mean – it must have been here a long time, right?"

"Since ze war, mademoiselle; it's a German officer," another man says.

I locate my phone and begin to call the police. "What are you doing?" Xavier asks, looking ashen.

"Ringing the police of course."

"Perhaps we should dig a bigger 'ole and re-bury ze poor man, let 'im rest in peace, yes?"

"Certainly not! I have to report this, Xavier. What are you thinking?" He shakes his head and begins to walk away, so I shout, "Come back, you found him. They will want to speak to you."

"Truthfully, ze contractors found 'im, I just 'appened to be 'ere," he says shrugging. What is his problem now?

This time, several vehicles arrive at speed with their sirens screaming; announcing trouble to the whole village. The police officer in charge immediately separates us, assigning an individual officer to take a statement from each person involved, while a separate team rapidly constructs a tent over the victim and the area is cordoned off. Another unmarked vehicle arrives, containing what looks like a team of forensic scientists wearing white hooded suits who disappear into the tent. Sometime later, Xavier, I and all four of the workmen are asked to supply a DNA sample and are then instructed to leave.

"Is it a body from the war?" I ask before leaving.

"We have no way of knowing until forensic tests have been carried out. In the meantime, no more work can be carried out at this site. Also, you must not discuss this with anyone," the detective says, "you are witnesses in a potential murder investigation."

"You don't think we did this, do you?" I ask, somewhat shocked.

"It's a routine procedure, Mademoiselle. We don't know anything yet."

A small crowd of local people and guests from the campsite have gathered on the field along with members of the press, and an officer is swiftly dispatched to deal with them. Xavier and I visit each of our guests, reassuring them that it should not interfere with their stay.

Back at the Chateau, Alice arrives after school with Gus in tow, looking concerned, and wanting to know the story, which we recount with the scant details that we have. She keeps looking at Xavier with a strange expression and jumps when the landline rings. "Don't answer it," she snaps.

"Why?" I ask, standing up. "What if it's potential clients?"

"No doubt it will be busybodies, fishing for information," she replies, looking at Xavier with a disturbed expression. The ringing phone stops.

"Mama, take Gus 'ome. I will stay 'ere wiz Laura tonight."

Alice nods and ushers Gus out.

Mm, not a good idea. I don't want to be alone with Xavier. I find him impossible to resist, so I say, "No one is going to be stupid enough to try and break in tonight with police crawling all over the place; you spend some time with your family."

He looks around to make sure Gus isn't nearby, then places his hand on my small bump and whispers in my ear, "You and zis baby are family."

"Dad, are you ready? Oh, what are you doing?" Gus asks as he walks back through the door into the kitchen.

"Tell him," I urge as Xavier jumps away from me.

"Tell me what? Dad, what should you tell me?" Gus asks with a look of pure innocence and curiosity on his face.

Alice is now behind him, witnessing the uncomfortable scene. "Gus, your father has something to tell you. Let's all sit down for a few minutes," she says, gesturing to the table.

"What is it, Dad? Are you ill? One of my friends at school, his dad has had a heart attack," Gus says, now looking concerned.

"No Gus, I'm not ill; we're all fit and well. You know zat Laura is having a baby?"

Gus nods then asks, "Is the baby ill?"

"Erm, no, the baby's fine, Gus. I've got a photo of it here," I say, taking the image off a shelf in the kitchen.

Gus takes it from me and looks at the image then looks back to me, "Cool, is it a boy or girl?"

"It's too early to tell, son," Xavier says, then continues, "Laura's baby is also, erm, my baby; it will be your brother or sister."

Gus puts the photo down on the table and looks at Alice. He says, "Nana, I think we should go now." Looking bemused, he picks up his school bag and walks through the back door. Alice gives Xavier a perplexed look then collects her things and follows Gus.

"Zat didn't go well," Xavier sighs.

"I think you should have told him earlier," I say, rubbing his shoulder. "Go on. You need to go and reassure him."

"'Ow?" Xavier runs his hand through his messy hair.

"Tell him that you will always love him, that he will always be an important person in your life. He needs to know that he's not going to be usurped by this baby."

"But zat is true. I will always love 'im…"

"Yes, you and I know that. But right now he needs to hear it from you; spend some quality time with him…"

"Doing what?" He asks, almost as child-like as Gus.

"I don't know. Go off camping together at the weekend, or fishing. Bonding. Now go home."

"But I don't want to leave you wiz zis mess," he says, pointing in the direction of the tent illuminated in the distance.

"For heaven's sake, go! I'm a big girl," I say, leaving the room.

18

I look out of my bedroom window early the next morning to see only one police car, and two men are dismantling the tent. They must have taken the remains away in the night. Shortly after breakfast, a uniformed officer calls in to inform me that they have completed their work onsite and tells me that we can't continue with our drainage works until further notice. My phone rings in my pocket, the annoying ringtone telling me it's Xavier.

"Laura, did you see Gus?"

"No, he went home with you…"

"'E's not 'ere. I went to wake 'im for school and 'e wasn't in 'is bed. I've looked everywhere."

"Jesus! Was he upset? He seemed different when he left last night…"

"'E was quiet, went to bed and zen wasn't in bed zis morning."

"The police have just left; perhaps you should ring them…"

"No. I don't want to make a fuss; zat would make it worse."

"Have you rung the school to see if he's there?"

"I'll do zat now," he says and cuts me off. Poor Gus, it was probably quite a shock for him. He's always seemed a happy, laid back sort of child. He never knew his mother, but Alice has been a great substitute. Poor Alice, she will be beside herself. Should I ring her? No, I'll go over. She was acting strange last night too. I arrive to find her sat at the table with a hankie in her hand.

"Oh Alice, is there anything I can do?"

"He's at school," she says, dabbing her red eyes.

"Oh, thank goodness, is he okay?"

"Xavier has gone over to talk to the headmaster. What a morning!"

"Poor Gus, this is all my fault…"

"No. It's not. Xavier should have told him earlier. If anything, it's my fault."

I sit down beside her and hug the kind-hearted woman that I consider to be my surrogate mother. "Oh Alice, he'll come around; it was just a bit of a shock for him. I don't want him to feel left out. He means the world to me, as do you and Xavier. We'll sort this out."

"What should we do?"

"Well, I don't have any experience of parenting, but I suggest we stand back and give him space and time. When he's ready, we need to have a chat," I say.

"Will he live at the Chateau with you, Xavier, and the baby?" Alice asks, taking me by surprise.

"Alice, I have no idea how things are going to turn out; it's still early days. I don't think that even I know what I want…"

"Xavier adores you; he always has. I know he has a funny way of showing it at times. He's like that with Gus. He finds it difficult to show emotion."

"Well, he needs to tread gently with Gus. Spend more time with him and less time with me."

"But you need him, and there's work…"

"Right now, Gus needs him more. I can manage for a weekend. See if you can talk him into going camping, or something."

"What about the police and the body? Nasty business," she says, looking uncomfortable.

"Oh, they've removed it. The detective said it would be at least a week before we hear anything, nothing he can do about that. I'm not worried; it's unquestionably some remains from the war. Who knows, there may be others…"

We both look over to the door as Xavier arrives, looking relieved. "Is he okay?" Alice asks, jumping to her feet.

"I didn't see 'im, but ze teacher said 'e arrived at school at 7 am, and zey gave 'im breakfast. I'm going to get 'im at 'ome time. Silly boy…"

"Xavier, he's still a child. He's feeling pushed out…"

"Yes! You are taking him camping on Friday. I will get you the equipment from the scouts," Alice says firmly.

Xavier opens his mouth to object, but a stern look from me silences him.

"Okay, I'll leave you two to get on," I say, turning to leave.

"No, I'll leave you two to talk," Alice says, pointing to the chairs at the table. Xavier and I both sit. "I'll put the kettle on the stove then go and meet my friend." She fills the kettle and prepares the cafetière with ground coffee, then places some mugs in front of us. Oh no! Now, what am I supposed to say? Xavier and I sit in uncomfortable silence as the kettle begins to boil. "I'll be back in time for Gus.

I'll come with you to collect him," she adds to Xavier as she plonks the coffee on the table and leaves.

"Erm, so what is it zat we are supposed to be talking about?" Xavier asks when she's gone.

"The future, I believe. Your mother asked me if Gus would be moving into the Chateau with you and the baby." Xavier half chokes on his coffee and begins to cough. "So, talk," I add.

Once his breathing returns to normal, he takes my hand and says, "Sorry."

"Sorry for what, exactly?"

"Mama; she can be blunt at times, but she 'as a point. Gus needs to know where he stands." He rises from his seat and walks purposefully around the table to sit in the empty chair beside me then continues, "What do you want to do?"

"Honestly? I have no idea. I have given it a lot of thought. You can't move in and leave Gus behind; if you bring Gus, that will leave Alice alone. And if all three of you move in, we'll have no bedrooms left for guests."

"You could move in 'ere…"

"It only has three bedrooms, and I don't want to leave the Chateau; who would look after the guests anyway?"

Frustration is written on his face as he runs his hand through his unruly hair. His features soften, and he leans forward and very quietly asks, "Do you not want to live wiz me?" That is the burning question, but I don't have an answer. I've written a list of pro's and con's numerous times, and I still don't know. I need to be tactful. My hesitation seems to be enough of an answer for him, and he continues, "I realise zis was not in your plans, but… I love you." He pauses and looks at me awaiting my response, but it isn't forthcoming, "I zink I loved you ze first time I saw you when you answered ze door in your

176

nightdress wiz your 'air looking like a birds nest..."

At last, I find my voice. "If I remember correctly, you were rude and belligerent. You didn't make me feel in the least bit welcome. What sort of love is that?"

"Yes, I know. I wanted to 'ate you, but you made it impossible, wiz your naivety and innocence. But you started to get under my skin. You were so kind and dedicated when Mama was ill, and your generosity when Gus needed 'elp..."

"Stop!" I say, slightly more firmly than I intended, though it has the desired effect. "Why did you want to hate me?"

"Ze Chateau, of course. Ze whole village assumed it would come to me..."

"Tell me honestly; is that why you want to move in with me?"

"No! It is not! I did try to stop you when you were seducing me after we 'ad been in ze 'ot tub—" I look into his worried face and laugh. His expression slowly changes into confusion. "What is so funny?"

"Oh, Xavier, you are," I say, placing my hand on his chest. "The simple truth is that I don't know what I want. It would be a mistake to rush into anything just because it's convenient. Yes, I'm expecting your baby, and no, I don't regret that now; it's growing on me. Literally. We need to have this conversation with Gus and Alice. Explain to them that in the future, we may well become a family. However, I don't want to cause upheaval in Gus's life until I'm sure. You once told me that you would wait…"

He lifts my hand from his chest, places the tips of my fingers to his lips and plants a kiss on each one. "I can live wiz zat," he says. He hesitates, and looks into my eyes before asking, "Erm, do you 'ave feelings for me?"

I place a gentle kiss on his lips. "Yes, you know I do, but you drive me crazy. I don't know if I want to shout at you or jump into bed with you."

"Number two sounds better," he adds with a relieved laugh.

"Well, I'm going now to prevent myself from doing just that. Let me know how Gus is when you collect him. We'll talk when he's ready," I say and make my escape.

19

I get back home to find yet another small van outside the Chateau. I grab my phone as I approach and take a quick photo of the number plate and the man dressed head to toe in khaki; just in case. "Can I help you?" I ask.

"Bonjour Mademoiselle, I am Jacques Bonnet. I heard about the body on the local radio and…"

"I'm sorry, Monsieur, you are wasting your time. I'm not at liberty to discuss the matter. It is an ongoing police investigation."

"No, Mademoiselle. I'm not interested in gossip either. My hobby is metal detecting, and I would like to investigate your land." His comment throws me, and I stand and stare at him, slack-jawed. He continues, "It's common knowledge that you have previously found items hidden in your property, so the chances are that there may be objects of value buried in the grounds."

"Oh, erm, I've never thought of that."

"The body, for instance. I would have been able to find it because of the metal items discovered alongside it."

"Mm, but I'm not sure that the police would allow it at the moment."

"They don't need to know, Mademoiselle. I would be discrete and start at the other side of the estate, away from the area where they discovered the body," he adds, looking somewhat confident. He has a point, but I'm not sure that I want him to find yet another body or more unexploded ammunition. "I can see that you need more time to consider this. Ring me," he says, handing me a professional-looking business card.

Once he's gone, I get straight onto the internet to research metal detecting. It seems that generally, the landowner and detectorist must share any objects of value, and declare any items of historical interest. "What do they consider to be of historical interest?" I ask, but Shadow takes no notice of my ramblings. "Do I need permission or a license?" I find the answer quickly. I only require the landowner's permission. Well, that's easy enough. If the finds are considered to be archaeological artefacts, then they must be reported to the Territorial Commission. In which case, they will automatically belong to the French State. If not, the landowner and detectorist should share the finds equally.

"Well, that's a rather ambiguous law," I say, but Shadow carries on sleeping, seemingly disinterested. Hmm, who or what are the Territorial Commission? A question for Monsieur le Maire, I think. I'll send Alice a text.

Sorry to bother you, I was wondering if you could ask Monsieur le Maire a question for me the next time you see him? X

A short while later, she replies.

What a coincidence. I've just bumped into him. What would you like to know? X

Coincidence? Mm, I wonder.

I want to know what permission I need to perform metal detecting on the estate, do I need to declare my finds? Who are the Territorial Commission? P.S. Give him my regards. X

It's early evening before I get my reply.

He says that you only need to declare artefacts that are of significant archaeological interest. There are some restrictions. You can't search battlefields and the northern beaches, where you may come across unexploded ammunition, but you should be fine on the estate. X

It's still somewhat ambiguous. When does an object become an artefact? And, it's not like I'm going to come across any medieval treasure, or a hoard of Roman coins is it? Okay, so how much does this equipment cost and where can I get it? I'll research it in a minute but need to respond to Alice's text.

Thank you. How's Gus? X

Poor Gus, I hope he's okay.

Better, and he's sorry. Xavier has taken him out with the dogs. Why do you want to know about metal detecting anyway? X

That's good news, so I send a quick response before heading back to my research.

Long story, I'll explain later. X

The prices vary enormously, and I know nothing about metal detectors. More research and a discussion with Xavier is required then.

Days turn into weeks, with still no news about the body. Although I am anxious to know the identity of the man and the reason for his burial on my land, the police continue to fob me off when I contact them. At least we have been allowed to complete the drainage ditch. Other than that, life flows along like a lazy river, without further significant incidents.

I'm pleased to see that Xavier is spending more time with Gus. With a little nudge from me, he's invested in a second-hand metal detector, and Gus enjoys going out with him and the dogs. "*It is good training for ze puppies too,*" he insists, though they are hardly puppies anymore. They haven't found much of interest, apart from a bent earring on the lawn in front of the Chateau; it is gold, set with a beautiful diamond. I wonder who it belonged to, and where the other one is? Was it lost in a moment of passion under the stars? I guess we'll never know. Gus has researched it and thinks it's from the 1920s. He was excited when he brought it to me, and I told him 'finders' keepers.'

Xavier is miffed because all he's found so far is old nails and rusty cans, but it's lovely seeing them so happy together. I don't know if they've discussed the baby or the future in detail, but Gus seemed accepting when we had a family chat. It's early July and getting too hot for me. I'd love to immerse my rotund body in the hot tub, but pregnant women aren't supposed to use them. I wish we had a pool.

20

Sixteen weeks today and I'm indulging myself. Sweet Pea is now the size of a cupcake. They weren't joking when they said, 'a cupcake is for life and not just for birthdays!' At least I know she has chocolate frosting and not red velvet. Will she have my non-descript grey eyes or beautiful round chocolate buttons like her French family?

All this thought of food is making me hungry. I'm trying to snack on fruit and vegetables, as I'm starting to get quite round, but it's not so simple with Alice bringing her fresh baking over most days. Only three weeks until my next scan, then they will be able to identify its gender. Xavier doesn't want to know, but I'm sure she's a girl. I've thought so ever since I saw her first grainy image. Do I want to know? I'm not sure. I suppose it will be simpler for knowing what colour clothes to buy. Alice is already busy knitting. I haven't bought anything yet. It's too early, and I've been extremely busy with work. Talking of work, Alice and I are meeting with the caterers later today. It's the rally in two weeks; I need to get a move on.

I return to find an official-looking letter in the letterbox. It seems urgent, but first, I need to get out of these restrictive clothes and into something more comfortable. The air has become humid, and I feel hot and sticky. I'd love to go for a swim just now, but a refreshing shower will have to suffice.

A short while later, feeling a little fresher, I sit down with some ice-cream and open the letter. It's brief and only states that the human remains found on the estate have been dated to the war and therefore concludes the criminal investigation. Is that all I get? Who was he and how did he die? Have his family been informed? How can I find out? It's so frustrating! A phone call to the police draws a blank. They can't divulge personal information, and I find nothing on the internet to point me in the right direction.

Hunger halts my research. Gherkins, I need a gherkin sandwich, and I need it now. A rummage through the cupboards proves fruitless. Pickled onions will have to do. I munch my way through half a jar before making myself stop, followed by more ice-cream, vanilla and lavender this time. It's one of Alice's experiments, and I love it. Once full, I take a photo of the letter and send it to Alice, who replies immediately.

Thank goodness for that, it's one less thing to worry about! X

Hmm, I wonder why she was so concerned? Perhaps I should walk over to see her. I look out of the window to see that the sky has darkened, taking on the now-familiar purple shades of a severe bruise — that can only mean one thing. A mighty storm. Not a good time to go out, so I make myself comfortable on the window-seat in the dining room. I watch the sky as lightning illuminates it, followed shortly by thunder's low rumbling noise. I remember the first storm I witnessed here, almost a year ago now. I don't know what I was thinking by hanging out of the window in my nightdress, trying to close the shutters. I woke up in a pool of water, with Xavier pouring brandy into my mouth. Yuk.

The rain starts, slowly at first but I know what's coming. I jump up and discard my clothes in anticipation. By the time I reach the back door, it's coming down like stair rods, as my gran used to say. I rush over to the long grass at the other side of the backyard, now only in my underwear, and let the rain cascade over my swollen body. It feels cathartic. I hold my arms out wide and twirl around slowly in a circle with my eyes closed.

"Are you crazy?" A familiar voice whispers in my ear. "You are soaking."

I open my eyes to find Xavier stood with his hands on his hips and his overly long hair stuck to his face. "So are you," I laugh.

He steps closer, and his eyes find mine. "You look beautiful," he says.

"I think you need to get your eyes tested. I'm fat."

"No, you are not! You're just keeping ze baby warm," he says, taking hold of my hand.

"Well, she's too hot, and now I'm cooling her down," I say, putting my arms around his neck and drawing him closer.

"Let's take zis inside."

"No," I say, watching disappointment cloud his face. "Make love to me out here." His smile returns then he carefully lays me down on the wet grass and frees my large, sensitive breasts to the elements before removing his soggy clothes. Out of the corner of my eye, I witness a praying mantis devour an unfortunate cicada, headfirst, but it's not enough to put me off as the first wave of pleasure pulsates through my body. It's a good job we don't have any guests tonight!

The storm rumbles on into the night, and I send Xavier home to be with his family and immerse myself in a refreshing bath. Laid on my bed a while later, I think back over my time here in the Ardèche. In two weeks, I will have been here for a whole year. It's gone so quickly, and I've achieved so much with the help of Xavier, Alice, and the local community. I'm a different person as well as about to become a mother. I try to think forward a year from now, what will life be like then? I'll have an eight-month-old baby to care for as well as a Chateau and business to run. I genuinely do need to make some decisions. I can't float along in this state of non-commitment for much longer. But what do I want? I already know the answer. However, how can I make it happen?

I want Xavier and Gus to move in here with me, but I can't leave Alice out. Moving them all in would use up too many of the guest bedrooms, and I don't think Alice would consider leaving the farmhouse anyway; she's lived there ever since she got married. We could convert the attic as Xavier suggested once before, but I don't have the funds for that. It seems ironic, I have a six-bedroomed Chateau but don't have enough room for my ready-made family. I won't, of course, share this information with them yet. Not until I've figured out a way to make it work.

Walking across to the campsite the following morning, I'm relieved to find that the new drainage ditch has worked well, preventing the field from flooding again. On my way back I pass Xavier and his cousin Bert, laying new gravel where the rally cars are going to park. Both men wave as I pass by, but I don't stop, I've got rooms to prepare.

Life becomes a frenzy of activity, but at last, the big event looms. Only one more day to go, and all of the rooms are full. I'm waiting for my remaining guests to arrive. Xavier accepted the booking, but all it says in the diary is Dino plus one, and he's booked the best room. I don't have long to wait before I see a little blue car making its way down the drive. It stops outside, and a man wearing designer labels gets out and retrieves expensive-looking luggage out of the small car boot. An elegant looking woman gets out of the driver's seat and turns to wave. Oh, my

God, it's Valentina! She casually saunters over, removing her leather gloves and designer shades while doing a double-take, "Look at you!" She says, moving closer for a hug. "I didn't know you were expecting. Is Enzo here?"

I shake my head. "And I didn't know you were coming, why didn't you tell me?" I say, deflecting her question.

Valentina smiles and introduces me to her companion, "Dino, this is my friend Laura."

His masculine features break into a smile before saying, "Laura, pleased to meet you at last; I've heard all about your achievements."

"Yes, but this is one achievement I didn't know about," Valentina says, pointing to my bump, "when are you due?"

"I'm only eighteen weeks, so a while to go yet."

"Nearly half-way through now, it will pass very quickly," Dino adds.

"Let me show you to your room. You should have told me you were coming. You didn't need to book."

"Yes, that's why I didn't tell you; we're just regular guests and don't want to put you to any extra trouble." She adds, "Is there anything we can do to help?"

"Certainly not, I don't expect my guests to work. Besides, I've taken on extra staff for the event. Are you competing?"

"Goodness, no, my little car isn't old enough; it's classic but not vintage. I'm looking forward to spectating tomorrow, though."

"Me too. Please join us for a drink after dinner this evening," I say, handing the key to the room to Valentina before heading back to the kitchen to help Alice.

21

The marshals and officials arrive early to prepare the area where the special driving test is to take place. Xavier has made an effort and for once looks quite presentable in his crisp white shirt and smart trousers; he's even wearing a waistcoat and has had his hair cut for the occasion. Gus has been allowed to take the day off school and has set up a small enterprise, selling home-made ice-cream to the marshals and spectators that have gathered.

A cameraman arrives first before the drivers and navigators begin to trickle in for lunch, and I have front-of-house duties once more — standing at the entrance to the marquee and greeting them as they arrive. Monsieur Le Maire is strutting about enjoying the attention, that is when he's not following Alice around like a puppy-dog. I become aware of clapping and cheering outside as I'm greeting more lunch guests. "Where is she?" I hear Valentina ask in the distance. Does she mean me? I pop my head outside to find her walking towards the marquee, accompanied by a middle-aged man with a stomach to rival mine. "There you are! I'd like you to meet Charles, a friend of the family," she says.

He leans forward for the traditional kiss on each cheek, "Enchanté, Mademoiselle."

"Hello Charles, I'm Laura; pleased to meet you. I trust you are enjoying the event?"

"Yes, very much; thank you for hosting the lunch halt."

"Do come and look at Charles's car," Valentina says.

"Oh, erm, I'll need to find someone to take over from me."

"Already sorted," says Dino as he appears from nowhere and stands beside me.

Valentina leads me through the small crowd that has gathered. I'm surprised by how much interest there seems to be over a bunch of wealthy middle-aged men driving around in old cars; but hey, it's good for business. When I get to the front, I recognise the local journalist, who starts taking photos of me. Great, I'm going to appear in the local newspaper like an advert for rent-a-tent.

Charles's car is a small blue and black one with sweeping wheel arches. Charles takes my hand and says, "Let me help you in." I squeeze my body into the passenger seat, still not aware what all the fuss is about as he continues, "She's a beauty, isn't she? Thank you."

Puzzled, I ask, "Erm, thank you for what?"

"Selling her to me."

"What? Wait a minute – this is the old Bugatti?" I smile. "Oh, my God! I didn't recognise her." I sit in stunned silence while Charles climbs in beside me and starts her up with a loud clattering whine, which takes the smile off my face.

"Don't be alarmed, it's only the supercharger," he says as the crowds part, and we leave the parking area. My eyes find Xavier, Alice, and Gus waving in the crowd as we drive off towards the front gate. Unquestionably, they were a party to this. I look up to see a drone following us between the trees.

Any conversation is futile with the sound of the engine and the wind whipping my hair about, so I immerse myself in fantasy — imagining that I'm a lady of some importance going for a ride into the countryside. I wonder how many times this old car has driven up here and who she's carried? Did the mysterious lady, who lost the diamond earring that Gus found, travel in her?

All too soon we return, but Charles doesn't turn into the carpark as I expect but carries on to the front door of the Chateau, where a photographer is waiting. Xavier steps forward and assists me out of the cramped seat. Charles climbs out, and steps to the side as Xavier and I are asked to pose by the car. The photographer gets to work at once, with my hair once again looking like a bird's nest, then realisation dawns — this is a recreation of the old photograph of the Bugatti outside the Chateau, which has pride of place in the drawing-room. Now I can add another layer of history and put this by its side.

"Thank you," I whisper into Xavier's ear.

"Don't zank me; it was Valentina's idea." I look over to my dear friend and smile, unable to stop the tears from blurring my vision.

The rest of the afternoon is spent watching the old cars whizzing around the cones in the farmyard area before they disappear, bouncing up the rear driveway in clouds of dust to continue onto their next venue.

"I can't believe how they treat these valuable old cars. I would expect the owners to wrap them in cotton-wool."

But Valentina disagrees, "They were built to be driven, not cosseted."

The marshals have everything tidied away in record time, and the old Chateau falls eerily silent once again. Valentina and Dino climb into their little blue car and follow behind them, promising to be back for dinner, and I also bid farewell to my other guests who had stayed the night. "You must be exhausted, go and 'ave a rest," Xavier says, putting his arms around me.

"But I've got the guest rooms to service, and dinner to prepare for this evening," I reply.

"Zat was an order; not a request. Zere are enough of us to cope wizout you for a while. Go!" He insists, patting me on my bottom. I admit that I'll be glad to get these tight shoes off and put my feet up for a while.

22

Like sleeping beauty, I awake with a kiss; and a cup of tea. "What time is it?" I ask, looking up at my prince.

"It's 6.20 pm, you've got time for a shower."

"Are you going to join me?"

Xavier looks at me with a mischievous smile then says, "We'd be late for dinner if I did," then turns to leave.

I told Valentina and Dino that I'd make dinner for 7.30 pm. It's an informal affair, so I dress in a canary yellow sundress and pull on a loose white, lacey blouse, which resembles a cobweb to cover my ample cleavage.
Concern creeps over me when I reach the top of the staircase, and I can't smell food cooking. Dinner should be ready by now. I become even more alarmed when I find

Valentina and Dino chatting to Xavier in the drawing-room, they are all wearing their finery. What's going on?

"You look lovely, Laura; please excuse us for a moment," she says, exiting the Chateau via the front door. Watching them leave, I poke my head into the kitchen to find it devoid of life.

"Where is Alice, and what's for dinner?" I ask, my voice raising an octave.

"I'm taking you out for dinner," Xavier replies, tucking my hand into the crook of his elbow then quietly whispering, "You look radiant."

"I don't feel radiant…"

My words halt as we step out of the front door. I stand and stare as I look over to the marquee, now festooned with fairy lights and flowers. Xavier leads me forwards and gives a fake-sounding cough as we reach the closed opening. Two young men from the village step forward and lift the flaps, securing them with coloured ribbons, and Xavier guides me inside. A tremendous cheer, followed by clapping, reverberates around the big tent. I can hardly believe my eyes. A sea of colour and faces stare back at me, familiar faces, but my mind can't process any more information for the time being. I feel like I'm in a trance as Xavier leads me to the top table and takes his place by my side, assisting me into a chair.

As I sit down, Monsieur Le Maire on my right follows suit, which the crowd then copies. You could hear a pin drop, and I realise all eyes are on me. Forcing myself to concentrate, I gaze around. Gus sits on Xavier's left, and Alice is seated next to Monsieur Le Maire. Valentina and Dino stand out at their table, as they're wearing immaculately made clothes, then I notice Jacques with Jenny at his side sitting with them. Oh, my God! When did she arrive? I'll kill her. We only spoke a couple of days ago.

Monsieur Le Maire breaks the spell by standing up. "Ladies and gentlemen, thank you for attending this special dinner to celebrate the anniversary of Laura's first year in France."

I struggle to concentrate on his words of wisdom as I continue my search of the crowd. John and Jackie Burrows are sitting with Sylvie and her family. The big tent is full of local people. Yvette is sitting with the village doctor and his wife. Monsieur Bertrand and his wife are sitting with Madam Cevert and her husband; the list is endless. How did I not know about this?

I sit frozen to my chair as the crowd stands and raises their glasses. Monsieur Le Maire smiles down at me and says, "A toast... to Laura, for all of her hard work throughout this past year, sympathetically restoring this Chateau to its former glory and creating much-needed employment for the village. To Laura," he finishes.

The crowd echoes his sentiment, followed by the chants of "Speech!"

Oh, my God, I'm in no fit state to string a sentence together, so a coherent speech is out of the question. Anyway, what would I say other than 'thank you for coming'? I dig Xavier in the ribs, and he squeezes my hand and stands, taking a crumpled piece of paper out of his pocket. "I'd like to follow by, first of all, zanking everyone for coming. Some of you have travelled quite some distance to get 'ere," he coughs nervously then continues, "it's been a long and at times fraught journey for Laura to get to zis point, but I assure you, she wouldn't want it any ozer way. She adores ze Chateau and ze community in which it resides." Monsieur Le Maire stands and claps as Xavier sits back down, and the crowd cheers once more. I clutch Xavier's arm, willing the tears not to fall. He is incredible, and I know I have to find a way to make this work. I can't imagine life without this loving man and his family at my side. Monsieur Le

Maire gives the signal to serve dinner, and the servers get to work, like an army of ants, serving the starters. I can't help but laugh as a young woman discreetly places a dish of pickled gherkins near my plate.

After dinner, Jacques and his friends make their way to the corner of the marquee where musical instruments are set up. Gus surprises me by joining them, taking his place at the piano. Xavier takes my hand and guides me through my guests to the dance floor, as once again, all eyes are on me. Jenny winks and gives me a thumbs-up as Xavier takes me in his arms and whirls me around the dancefloor. When did he learn to waltz? The hairs stand up on the back of my neck, and my skin prickles — the familiar tell-tale signs that Aunt Mary is watching. Camera's flash but soon everything fades into oblivion. I only have eyes for this amazing man in my arms.

23

A joint effort the next morning produces a buffet-style breakfast in the formal dining room. Enthusiastic chatter fills the building as old friends catch up.

"I can't believe you managed to surprise me again," I scold as Jenny appears shamelessly late for breakfast. She only sticks her tongue out at me and heads for the coffee pot.

When the band emerges bleary-eyed from their sleeping bags, Gus says, "Don't worry, we've saved you guys some." They shuffle to the table to make their choices.

Monsieur Le Maire keeps a low profile, which is so out of character and is the first to leave shortly after breakfast. I look out of the big window to witness him and Alice snatch a tender moment before he climbs into his car. I wonder where he slept. Oh, that must be the reason why Gus slept in my room with Xavier and I and not with Alice! They make an unlikely couple, but I'm thrilled that she has him in her life. Valentina and Dino are next to leave, with promises of keeping in touch. Sadly, the Burrows had a plane to catch midmorning, having left their three children with grandparents for the night, so left just after Valentina and Dino. Lunchtime rolls around and only Jenny and Jacques remain.

"Sorry to be a party pooper, I've got to get back to work," Jacques says.

"But it's Saturday!" Gus exclaims.

"Saturday it might be, but I've got cars to mend," he replies, ruffling Gus's hair. "I'll pick you up at eight," he adds to Jenny, dropping a kiss on her head.

"What's the plan for the rest of the day?" Jenny asks.

"I'll have the marquee to tidy after…"

"It's your weekend off. Ze work is taken care of; Mama, Sylvie, and her family will sort everyzing. You can 'ave a lazy day wiz Jenny," Xavier responds.

"What are we going to do, Dad?" Gus asks. "Can we take the metal detector out?"

Xavier shrugs, so I quickly say, "What a good idea, Gus," then enquire after the puppies.

"Patch is perfect. Dad says he can be my dog," he replies, beaming. "Pepper is quite good, and Dad's going to sell him, but Freckles – well, I don't know what we're going to do with him."

I look from father to son and wonder what they're thinking, "'E's not good enough to sell, and it won't be easy to find 'im a new 'ome…"

"Don't you dare! I'll have him, there's plenty of room for him here," I say, giving Xavier a hard stare.

"I 'ad no intention of 'arming 'im – I wouldn't dare!" He replies with his hands held up in a gesture of surrender. "But, you will 'ave your 'ands full soon."

"One more little dog won't make much difference, in the scheme of things," Jenny adds, coming to my defence, then looks at me and exclaims, "We're going baby shopping!"

"Oh, it's too early…"

"Rubbish! You're nearly half-way there; you've got to start sometime."

"There isn't much choice in town, only the department store and a couple of designer mother and baby boutiques that cost the earth. Besides, I won't need much."

"You will be surprised by how much you're going to need; let's look online and make a list," Jenny says, taking control of my laptop.

By early afternoon, Jenny's wish-list is longer than a country mile. "I'm beginning to wonder whose baby this is. Yours or mine?" I complain.

"Definitely mine, but you can do the difficult bits, like giving birth and night feeds," she says with a grin. "Seriously, I want to be involved, but I'd rather not have to perform an emergency delivery as we did with Jackie!"

"I'll second that. I'm having an epidural for sure. I've got a scan booked next week, Xavier is so excited."

"Oh, it's a shame I've got to go back tomorrow; send me a photo. Have you chosen any names?"

"I'd love to call her after my gran, but Florence doesn't do it for me."

"Mm, me neither, but it's better than Sweet Pea. Anyway, how do you know it's not a he?"

"Gut instinct. What's wrong with Sweet Pea?"

"You need to keep an open mind. Then you won't be disappointed if it's a boy. What does Xavier want?"

"Oh, he'll want a boy for sure, someone to help on the estate. That's how it works here, but, of course, he hasn't said that. It's not going to be plain sailing though, whatever the baby turns out to be. His idea of parenting won't be anything like mine. We can't even agree on how to train a puppy."

Jenny grins, saying, "He may have a hard shell, but he's got a soft centre. A little girl will have him wrapped around her little finger, you wait and see."

All too soon, Jacques arrives, and the pair head off to town leaving me with my cheese and gherkin omelette. I hear them return at some unearthly hour — cutting it fine as always. Jenny has a plane to catch after breakfast, and I don't expect that they got much sleep, yet she still looks stunning. I don't know how she does it, unlike me. I'm beginning to look like a dumpling.

"Text when you land," I call through the car window as Jacques spins the wheels of his car on the new gravel, heading off for the airport.

24

Life continues at its usual fast pace as the days evaporate like summer rain and I reach the half-way mark. I'm now twenty weeks. Sweet Pea is now more like a sweet potato, while my abdomen is attempting to look like a melon, but Xavier seems to like it. It's my scan this afternoon, and I'm beginning to feel anxious. Xavier and Alice want to know the gender of this little intruder, but I'm not sure. I think the only thing that will keep me going through labour is wondering if it's a girl or a boy. Or am I better off knowing, then at least if it's a boy I can get used to the idea? I can't imagine sharing a house with three males. I've always lived with females, first Gran, then Jenny and the girls. Imagine all that dirty laundry, sports kits, and work clothes, as well as the guest's linens. How am I going to cope?

"Are you ready?" Xavier asks, entering into the kitchen.

"Almost; I need water and a wee."

At the hospital, the wait is excruciating, but at last, they call my name, and I'm invited to lay on the couch. This time, the cold gel is a welcome relief from the afternoon heat. The first thing I see is the reassuring heartbeat. The technician seems to take a while recording measurements of its head and organs, but I don't mind. I can't take my eyes off the screen. The images are captivating. Sweet Pea seems so big now, I can see her in profile; she appears to have a dainty nose and is sucking her thumb. She can't possibly be comfortable scrunched up into such a small space; it's a good job we can't remember being in-utero. I allow my eyes to wander for a second and gaze at Xavier. He is wearing the biggest grin I've ever seen. The technician steals our attention when she asks, "So, mummy and daddy, do you want to know the gender of your baby?"

Time stands still, and I feel like I'm standing on the top of a cliff. Xavier looks at me expectantly, and my mind is made up as realisation dawns. I don't care whether it's a boy or a girl. I'm madly in love with this little thing that has wormed its way into my body. My heart swells, and my eyes blur with the sting of tears. "Yes," is my one-word answer.

"Are you sure?" Xavier asks. I nod as a tear of joy spills down my cheek. Xavier stands and dabs it with a tissue.

"It appears in all probability that you are having a little boy, look," she says, pointing to an area on the screen. Our son chooses this moment in time to kick out his little leg. She asks, "Can you feel that?"

"Yes. Yes, I can. I can feel the baby kick!" I say excitedly. "I've felt that before but thought it was only my tummy rumbling."

"Well, now you know it's your son, practising his football skills," she says. Xavier jumps up and hugs me, getting the sticky gel on his shirt, but he doesn't seem to notice. "I'll leave you alone for a moment," she adds.

After collecting the photos, Xavier sits and stares at them then turns to me and says, "I know you wanted a girl. I hope you're not too disappointed. We can always try again later."

"Erm, I think one will be enough for quite some time, thank you, and no, I'm not disappointed. I know I will love him equally as much; at least we can start to plan now. Let's go home and tell them."

"Mama has stored all of Gus's baby zings in ze attic. We can go through zem and decide what you want. She will be so excited to 'elp." I look at him and smile when he quickly adds, "but you can buy new zings too."

"I'm more than happy to save money and reuse what we can, but I want a new car seat; safety standards have changed somewhat in the last ten years."

When we arrive at the farmhouse, Alice rushes to the door, demanding, "Well?"

"The baby is fine Alice, here," I say, handing her a photo.

She scurries to the table and puts her glasses on and inspects the image. "Is it a girl or a boy?"

"Look at ze photo and tell us," Xavier says mischievously.

"It's a little boy, Alice," I say, putting my arms around her. Tears fill her eyes and collect on the inside of her glasses. She reaches into her apron pocket and produces a tatty tissue and smears the lenses, making them worse. Xavier takes her spectacles and runs them under the kitchen tap while she composes herself. "Are you okay?" I ask.

"Yes, yes," she says in between sniffs, "I'm so happy, I didn't think I'd live to see any more grandchildren after my stroke. You have done so much for us. How can I ever repay you?"

"Oh Alice, you have nothing to repay, you're like a mother to me," I say, passing her a clean tissue. We both look to the door as Gus arrives home from school.

"Why are you crying, Nana?"

Alice stands and walks over to him and puts her hand on his shoulder. "Because I'm happy," she says. "Laura is having a baby boy."

"Good, someone to play football with," he says casually, helping himself to the contents of the baking tin — the three adults blinking in surprise at his easy acceptance.

I shake my head in disbelief and say, "Anyway, I must dash. I've got four guests for supper this evening."

Xavier prepares to stand, "I'll come and 'elp…"

"No need, I'm on top of things. I'll see you tomorrow," I say, leaving Xavier to deal with his family. The walk home gives me time to

think. I find him so distracting at the moment.
I don't want to begin to rely on him either.
I've always been fiercely independent, my gran
saw to that.

Later, I lay in bed and mull over the short-list
of names in my head, most of them were, of
course, girls names, but now I need to ditch
those and concentrate on all things male.
Hmm, French or English? I'm leaning
towards English, but perhaps that's not fair.
He will, after all, reside and go to school in
France. Will he speak only French? My
language skills are improving, but I've still got
a long way to go. I suppose I can learn with
him, that will be fun. Now I'm getting ahead
of myself — back to names. Xavier will want
something forceful and masculine like Charles
or Henri. I suppose they're bilingual, but
neither of them feels right to me. His father
was called Pierre, so I'm guessing that will be
on his list too. I should also stop calling the
baby Sweet Pea. That's going to be difficult.
What can I replace it with? My gran used to
call me sweetie-pie when I was behaving and
sunshine when she was irritated with me. I'm
not sure that either of those fit. I fall asleep

pondering the issue, and I awake to a bothersome noise. My alarm. I've got breakfasts to prepare.

25

After several busy days, I have the Chateau to myself again, bliss. Time to catch up with paperwork. My eyes regularly stray to the photo montage on my desk — three very different images of Sweet Pea. I should find a new name for him! His kicking is becoming stronger. Perhaps I should call him Striker. No, that doesn't sound right either. Knocking on the front door surprises me, and I wonder who it could be. Perhaps it's the postman.

"Adam, hello," I say as he steps into the hall. "Was I meant to be expecting you?" Adam was one of the men who helped refurbish the bedrooms when I first arrived.

He shakes his head. "No, I was passing," he says. "Are you busy?"

I take him into the kitchen and pour us both a cold drink, then sit at the table, "How can I help you?"

He looks back at me with a sombre expression before placing an envelope on the table, "I have received a letter. I thought you would be interested in its contents."

"Do you have a problem?" I ask, starting to worry for this sweet-natured man.

"Read it," he replies, as he passes me a piece of paper from the top of the small pile he pulls out of the envelope.

I open it and begin to read with trepidation.

Dear Monsieur Caron,

Please let me introduce myself. I am Hanna Schmidt, the niece of the German officer, Hans Weber, recently discovered buried in your village. I realise this is going to be a shock to you and your family, but I have evidence to prove that he is your grandfather. I have enclosed copies of the letters that your grandmother sent to his home address. She was unaware that he had died, murdered possibly by the local resistance, and must have thought that he had abandoned her. It was such a difficult time for everyone who lived through the war years, and I feel that it's now time to put the past behind us. You have a family in Germany that would be eager to make your acquaintance. Please contact me should you so desire.

Regards,

Hanna.

I look up to see Adam examining his hands in his lap. "Wow! What a shock, how did they find you?"

"It's complicated, but it was a close DNA match on a database in Germany."

"What do the other letters say?" I ask, pointing to the other pieces of paper.

Adam leans forward and runs his hand through his hair then leans back again, saying,

"It appears that my grandmother and this German officer were lovers. His unit withdrew from this area, and my grandmother was under the impression that he was safely back in Germany. She wrote to him several times, telling him she was with child, but never received a reply. How could he? He was dead and buried only a short distance away."

I sit and listen to this tale of unrequited love, and realise I'm so lucky to have Xavier to help me bring up this child. "So, the story about the… err… rape?"

"Just that, I guess," he says, a thoughtful frown on his brow. "A story that my great-grandparents made up to protect their daughter and her unborn, half-German child, but we'll never know for sure."

"So, what are you going to do now?"

Adam looks at me and shrugs. "I don't know," he replies, "If I meet these people, my grandmother's reputation will be tarnished, what will they think of me?"

"You once said to me before that it was time these stories needed telling before they are forgotten and lost forever. You are an amazing man. The locals will still respect you. You're still in shock, give it some time, and you might feel better. It would be a shame to spend the rest of your life, not knowing your true identity. I'll do anything I can to help. All you need do is ask, and I won't tell anyone." Adam nods and finishes his drink. I hesitate for a moment then ask, "While you're here, I was wondering if you would give me an informal estimate to have the attic converted into an apartment? Nothing fancy, just the plain necessities."

He looks back at me with a smile and replies, "Well, first, you would need a rough idea of what you want. How many bedrooms and bathrooms?"

"Erm, I'd like three bedrooms, if that's possible. One bathroom would be adequate and an open-plan living/kitchen area."

Adam nods and pops out to his van and comes back with a tape measure, notebook, and pencil, and we head up to the attic. He spends a while measuring and sketching in silence then sits on the floor in the central area and beckons me over, saying, "You could fit a spacious master bedroom with ensuite at the side with the balcony, plus a small family bathroom and three smaller bedrooms down the opposite side. Headroom would tail off near the outer walls, but you could use the space as storage. The central area would convert into a comfortable living area; it's very achievable. The windows are small, but there are enough of them."

"Wow!" I say, impressed. "That looks amazing, you are very talented, but how much would it cost?"

"I'd need to go away and work that out; it's quite a lot of work, but it's not structural. What about access? We'd need to improve that."

"Hmm, you can't remove the secret ladder that was in use during the war, it has to stay. Can you do anything with the other stairs that John discovered?" I ask, remembering the day that John knocked through to find a dangerous route into the attic. Once again, Adam sets to work, measuring and sketching, then looks back at me with a smile and a nod. "Excellent," I say. "I will need to have it done in stages; as and when I can afford it. Would that be a problem?"

"I will do my best to work on it when the weather is bad, when I can't do outside jobs. Then it will be a bit cheaper. I'll get back to you, and I won't tell anyone," he adds with a knowing look and a wink. Adam takes his leave, and I spend the rest of the day with a goofy grin on my face, imagining my new apartment, complete with family when I should be preparing for this weekend's wedding.

26

Week twenty-four and the foetus is now the size of a papaya and considered viable, should the unthinkable happen, and he hasn't got a name yet. I'm leaning towards Noah, but I haven't told Xavier. We need to sit down and have a discussion soon. I've had my pregnancy vaccinations, and the midwife wants me to write out a birth plan. I thought the idea was to get him out as quickly as possible, but it seems not. Being on the other side of things feels very different. In uniform, I felt confident and capable, but as a patient, I'm looking at all of the things that could go wrong. So, home birth is not for me. I want to be in a hospital where there is a backup should things not go to plan. Who do I want to be my birth partner?

Well, initially, I did think of asking Jenny. I know she will be here for the birth, but I don't want to push Xavier out. He has to be present at the birth of his son. I only intend to stay in hospital the minimum number of hours, assuming all is well with Noah. Noah. Yes, it's growing on me; it's a biblical name, so very multicultural. I want to breastfeed if I can. I've started leaking small amounts of milk already, so it shouldn't be a problem. I'm going to need a breast pump though, so Xavier and Alice can take a turn, especially at night!

I've got special guests this weekend. Hanna Schmidt and her daughter Angela, are coming to meet Adam and his family. I'm charging mates rates in return for work in the attic. The stairs are his first job, and he started on the project this morning. I still haven't told Xavier, but I won't be able to keep it a secret from him for much longer. Hanna wants to visit the site where her uncle Hans was discovered and place a memorial plaque in his honour. It's a lovely gesture, and I'm looking forward to learning more about this unfortunate man who was callously murdered and hidden on my estate about seventy-five years ago. The family have now buried his remains alongside his parents in Germany, where he belongs. The police don't appear interested in trying to discover who killed him. The perpetrators will undoubtedly be dead now anyway. I'm sure it's only one of many thousands of tragic stories from the war.

Xavier arrives as he sometimes does for lunch. "'Ave you got a problem?" He asks as he enters the kitchen, looking hot and sweaty.

"No."

"Zen, why is Adam 'ere?"

"Oh, just a small job that needed doing," I say airily.

"I am 'ere to do ze small jobs, you don't need to pay," he says, splashing his face with cold water from the utility room sink.

"The stairs up to the attic needed replacing. They were a bit dodgy. It had to happen at some point."

"Good idea, but I don't want you going up zere in your condition…"

"Xavier, I'm pregnant, not ill. Which reminds me, I have to write out a birth plan, have you got any suggestions?"

"Yes, drive to ze 'ospital, 'av ze baby and drive 'ome again," he says grinning.

"If only it were that simple, look what happened to Jackie."

With a sudden change of expression, he asks, "Will Jenny be 'ere?"

"I should think so, but I'd rather wait until I got to the hospital to give birth. In Jackie's case, it was her third child, and subsequent births are usually easier and quicker. Besides, I want an epidural." I say, then spot Adam as he appears at the kitchen door. "Adam, please join us for lunch."

"Oh, I don't want to intrude…" he replies, hesitating.

"Don't be silly. We can discuss what you would like me to make for dinner on Saturday evening when your guests arrive."

Xavier looks puzzled then asks, "Are you celebrating a special occasion?"

I look at Adam and realise I may have put my foot in it, so immediately think of an excuse on his behalf and say, "Erm, Adam has some old friends coming to stay for a couple of days—"

Adam looks at me sharply then interrupts, saying, "I have some family in Germany that I haven't previously met," he hesitates before continuing, "I have recently discovered that the German officer found on the estate was my grandfather."

Xavier stares at Adam in surprise, and Adam looks challengingly at Xavier, then Adam recounts the unfortunate story of Hans

Weber. Xavier's face clouds over as though he imagines the scene in his head. "It's a sorrowful tale, I'm sorry," Xavier says, looking uncomfortable before saying, "Sorry, I must go. Mama has asked me to do a small job zat I 'ave only just remembered."

What just happened? Xavier is usually more than happy to pass the time of day with the locals. What was so urgent that he had to leave his lunch behind? I'm not sure if Adam noticed the change in his demeanour, so I try to keep the conversation on the details about the renovation of the attic. I've paid him a thousand Euros upfront for materials, and he seems satisfied.

I don't hear from Xavier for the rest of the day. I wonder what he's been doing. I lay awake in bed, thinking about his reaction to Adam's news at lunchtime. I can't imagine that it has anything to do with his connection to having German lineage. The war was such a long time ago now, and the world is thankfully a different place. Noah decides to get his football boots on just as I'm dropping off to sleep, but it's still a novelty, so I roll onto my back and enjoy the contact.

The following morning dawns humid and sultry. Another storm looms. I get a call from Adam, telling me he's free to work in the attic as he can't continue with his other job in the storm. I can hear him banging about above me but don't go to investigate. I don't want to get in his way, but by lunchtime, the storm has passed, so he leaves to continue elsewhere. I enter the attic to find debris and tools strewn about, but the partition wall is down, creating a big space for the master bedroom.

I set about tidying the smaller pieces of rubble into a corner and place his tools to one side. Feeling a little dizzy, I sit for a while on his toolbox and survey the scene, trying to imagine the room completed. The sun, now directly overhead, is bathing the room with a golden glow through the roof light. It's going to be a fantastic space.

Just as I'm about to stand and leave, I notice
something glinting through a gap in the
skirting board where the wall has come down.
One of Adams tools must have got lodged
behind it. I make my way over, walking
carefully through the debris, and bend down
to try to retrieve the item, but it's wedged. I
wonder how it managed to get behind there? I
mooch about and find a claw hammer and
prize the old wood away from the wall. Once
the gap is wide enough, I slide my hand
behind, getting a nasty cut in the process. I'm
about to admit defeat when I feel something
about the size of a small phone. Now I'm
intrigued.

I persevere and pick the item up, but it's
heavy and drops from my fingers, back into
its dark recess. Looking around, I find a
lethal-looking chisel, which I wedge between
the wood and the wall, then give it a hard
wallop with the hammer. The wood splinters,
revealing its occupant. A shiny metal block. I
retrieve the object and sit on the floor to

examine it. I quickly put it down beside me as my brain finally works out what it is — a gold bar.

I decide that my eyes are playing tricks; lightning doesn't strike twice in the same place. I carefully pick it back up again and see a hallmark. What does it mean? And to who did it originally belong to? Was it hidden from the Germans during the war, like the other objects? How much is it worth, if it is indeed the genuine article, and what should I do with it?

Perplexed, I carefully carry it down to the kitchen and find my laptop. My favourite search-engine needs to know its weight, so I scurry to the cupboard to find my scales — one kilogram. Online, I could sell it for thirty-five thousand pounds. That will go a long way to refurbishing my new apartment! I slump into the nearest chair, feeling overwhelmed, quickly followed by a sense of guilt. Who hid it, and why didn't they come back to retrieve it after the war? I'm about to pour myself a stiff drink but stop myself in the nick of time.

It might be what I want, but it's not what Noah needs! I take a photograph of my newfound treasure, then slip it inside an old sock and place it in my underwear drawer. Perhaps I should invest in a safe.

27

My to-do list for the afternoon is now a distant memory as I wander from room to room pondering what to do. Should I tell Xavier or anyone for that matter? After all, it is mine, isn't it? Yes, I'll sell it and keep quiet. The last thing I need is for the press to get wind of it. That will only incite gossip and jealousy. It's taken me a long time to feel accepted by the locals. Perhaps I should donate some money to a village project. I'll make discreet enquiries.

Bedtime looms, but I feel restless. I'm way too hot, and my ankles are the size of Christmas puddings. I know that I ought to put my feet up but the fresh evening air beckons. There's no need for a torch under the voluminous full moon tonight. As I step outside, I can hear the stream rushing into the pond way over to my left, a legacy from the earlier storm. Instinctively, I make my way towards the noise with Shadow and Freckles at my side. As I get nearer, my steps become quicker, as though I'm a moth lured to a flame. I near my destination and discard my clothes along the way, arriving naked with a sense of freedom.

The water beckons, a silver ribbon under the massive moon, reminding me of a poem that my gran taught me when I was little called *Silver*, by Walter de la Mare.

> *Slowly, silently, now the moon*
>
> *Walks the night in her silver shoon;*

This way, and that, she peers, and sees

Silver fruit upon silver trees;

One by one the casements catch

Her beams beneath the silvery thatch;

Couched in his kennel like a log,

With paws of silver sleeps the dog;

From their shadowy cote the white breasts peep

Of doves in a silver-feathered sleep;

A harvest mouse goes scampering by,

With silver claws and a silver eye;

And moveless fish in the water gleam,

By silver reeds in a silver stream.

Resistance is futile. The moonlight guides me into the refreshing water. My swollen body tingles as the inky liquid envelops it. I sit immersed up to my neck as it swirls and eddies around me. Closing my eyes, I can see gold mixed with silver. I'm drunk, intoxicated by hormones and euphoria, how I love this corner of paradise.

My private swimming pool. Why didn't I think of this earlier? Gone is my mistrust of the creatures whose habitat I've entered, fish, frogs, and countless invertebrates. Back to nature, all of life sharing our one planet, a planet that we need to cherish. The estate is organic now. Xavier's father used fertiliser and pesticides in moderation, but Xavier stopped that practice when he took over from him, so I know the water is chemical-free. I let my mind wander and imagine an olive-skinned little boy splashing about beside me with his brightly coloured fishing net.

A tingle travels down my spine, and I slowly open my eyes to see the silhouette of a man, my man, sat a short distance away. "Are you going to join me?" I say. He only laughs and shakes his head, so I continue, "How long have you been there?"

"Long enough," he answers, before adding, "Is zis wise?"

"It's amazing, you should try it," I reply, standing and stretching my arms up to the moon, letting the cold-water stream off my body in rivulets of molten silver.

Xavier walks into the water and wraps a large towel around me, holding me close, saying, "Be careful, it's slippery 'ere, we don't want ze accident."

"How did you know where I was?" I ask as I step out onto the soft grassy bank.

"Ze dog; 'e came to get me."

"Shadow has been here all the time…"

"No, ze puppy; it seems 'e 'as a purpose after all."

"Freckles, his name is Freckles, and I'm very fond of him."

"Clearly, 'e is fond of you too. Come on; you need ze shower."

"Will you join me?"

The summer sun makes an early appearance the next morning, illuminating my bedroom. I'm hot, too hot, and I'm trapped. I open my eyes to find Xavier clinging to me like one of the vines that he cherishes, memories of last night's tender caresses come flooding back. Noah chooses this moment to do his workout. "Wake up," I whisper in Xavier's ear.

"What time is it?" He mumbles.

"Time to feel your son doing his press-ups," I say. He detangles himself in an instant, while I guide his hand to my melon-shaped abdomen.

"I can't feel 'im."

"Be patient. You will soon—"

I'm interrupted as Xavier shouts, "Yes, just zere. I felt 'im," I watch his face light up like that of a small child on Christmas morning. We lay like that for a while, until my stomach rumbles and Xavier dresses quickly before heading down to make breakfast.

"What was so urgent yesterday that made you forego lunch?" I ask when he returns bearing a tray, and I tuck into the toast and jam with the side order of pickles.

"Erm, nozing urgent. Mama wanted some wood chopping," he says before quickly heading out onto the estate. Now I know he's lying to me. There is a mountain of prepared logs in the coal house, and it's way too hot for a fire! But he's not the only one keeping a secret.

Once the door has closed behind him, my eyes alight on the top drawer where I've hidden mine amongst my underwear, should I take it into town to try and sell it? Perhaps I should keep it in a safe deposit box at the bank for security, but I can't use the village branch; I'm amazed it's survived. Most local branches back home have been turned into coffee shops. I can't sell the gold bar to the first person that offers me money. I need to take advice, but who can I trust? An image of Leo, Valentina's brother, comes to mind. He's sure to know of someone trustworthy that deals with this sort of thing; he is a Count after all.

The days pass, and my secret remains nestled between my Bridget Jones knickers and the wigwam like bras I now need to wear. I know I'm procrastinating, but there's no rush, is there? The apartment won't be ready for several months. Adam has done a couple of hours after work some evenings this week. Though he hasn't mentioned the damaged skirting board, and neither have I. Xavier thinks he's still working on the staircase. I don't know how to broach the subject. If I tell him that I'm following his suggestion and converting the attic, he will wonder from where I'm getting the money. I can't help wondering why Xavier is avoiding Adam. Adam's Aunt Hanna and cousin, Angela are coming today, and Xavier has decided to take the weekend off to go camping with Gus. He's definitely due some time off, and I'm pleased he's doing more with Gus, but it's out of character especially when we have guests.

28

Adam arrives early, offering to help but Alice has beaten him to it and is already busy in the kitchen, though she is quieter than usual. She would typically be quizzing me about the future and showing me the baby items that she's been knitting, but not today. It's all about work. Adam uses the time to continue in the attic while we prepare for our guests, who are driving down. They should be arriving at tea-time, having broken their journey last night at an unpronounceable town somewhere further north. "What is Adam doing up there?" Alice asks, not taking her eyes off her chopping board.

"I'm having some work done in the attic, as and when I can afford."

"What sort of work? He'll be making a lot of dust, and I've cleaned upstairs," she says, sounding irritated. "I don't know why he didn't go to Germany to visit these people, instead of having them here," she complains.

"They want to see where their uncle has been buried for all of these years and lay a plaque," I say, trying not to roll my eyes at her. "And, Adam is doing jobs that needed doing decades ago. He's sealed the door off with plastic sheets and is doing his best to prevent a mess, but yes, dust does get everywhere, Alice. Don't worry. I'll damp-wipe the stairs and landing after lunch."

Tea-time rolls around. Adam has gone home to change, and I, too, squeeze myself into a decent outfit and await their arrival. Alice prepares the kettle for tea while I walk out into the fierce sun to greet my guests. Hanna is a tall, lanky woman, approximately sixty-years-old and her daughter, Angela, looks about Xavier's age. Alice arrives with afternoon tea in the drawing-room, nods politely then retreats to the kitchen.

"I'm not used to these temperatures. I hope you don't think me rude if I go and have a rest. Do you have any air-conditioning?" Hanna says, wiping her brow with a white handkerchief.

"I'm afraid not, but the shutters are all closed, and the walls are thick. I think you will find it comfortable. If not, I can get you a fan," I contritely say.

Angels rolls her eyes, "Well, I love it, and I'm going in the hot tub."

I show the two women to their rooms and decide that a siesta is a good idea. It's going to be a long evening, and Adam and his family are due at 7 pm.

Voices outside alert me to their arrival, and I step out to greet them. Adam introduces me to his wife and two young daughters. He asks quietly, "What are they like?"

"To be honest, I've not seen much of them. Hanna spent most of the afternoon in bed, and Angela sat for an hour in the hot tub then went down to the village," I say. "They're both in the drawing-room now. Come and meet them." I lead Adam and his family to the drawing-room and say, "Ladies, this is Adam and his family." I then retreat to the kitchen to leave them to chat. I am, after all, only the hostess on this occasion.

As 7.30 pm approaches, I say to Alice, "Would you like to tell them that dinner is ready?"

"No, I'll serve, and you can waitress," she replies frostily.

"Alice, are you not feeling well?" I ask, but she doesn't answer, so I shrug and head to the drawing-room to let them know that the food is ready.

Adam's daughters, wearing identical pink dresses, steal the show for the first half of dinner and conversation appears to flow smoothly. My ears prick up when I hear the subject change. Hanna says, "It's tragic. Your grandmother clearly loved Hans. The letters she wrote to him convey her pain, especially the last one."

"I can't understand why his father didn't reply on his behalf," Adam says.

"He may well have, we'll never know. The last letter was dated mid-August 1944. It was a very turbulent time, culminating in the rapid retreat of the German army. It may well have been shambolic, with little time to prepare," she replies.

"Do you have a cause of death—" Adam begins to ask, but his wife interrupts him.

"Girls, shall we go and explore?"

I continue eavesdropping after the girls have been ushered into the drawing-room by their mother. "Allegedly, the poor man was executed. Shot at close range in the back of the head—"

"I'm going now. I've loaded the dishwasher," Alice interrupts from behind me, looking ashen.

"Yes, thank you for your help, Alice. Adam and his family are returning at ten in the morning to lay the plaque…"

"You don't need me for that," she says sharply. "It's a family affair," she adds frostily, leaving via the kitchen door.

How strange. I can't think what I've said or done to upset Alice like this. I toss and turn into the small hours searching my brain for anything that I may have done to cause Alice offence, but can't come up with anything. Sleep eventually takes over, and I wake up feeling groggy. I'm grateful that my guests only require a cold breakfast.

After escorting the small party over to the bank at the far side of the campsite, I give a brief explanation of events on that fateful day when the body was discovered by the contractors, then stand back. The area has not yet recovered from the excavation. The youngest of Adam's daughters suggests, "Daddy, let's plant some pretty flowers here."

"Yes, and some trees," the older one chimes, not to be outdone by her younger sibling.

Adam turns to me and asks, "Laura, would you mind?"

"I think it's a wonderful idea. If you tell me what you have in mind, I'll ask Xavier…"

"Truthfully, I'd like to do it myself, if that's okay?"

"Sure, I'll go back and prepare coffee and cake while you discuss it," I add, making my exit. It feels so awkward being here without Xavier and Alice; it is part of their history rather than mine. But it is my future, and I'm now custodian so I must deal with it. I leave my guests to continue swapping life stories and, after lunch, show them into the small museum housed in the library and sing Adam's praises about the craftsmanship of the cabinets that he built for me. As I turn to leave my eyes land on the book of memoirs written by Pere Flory, the priest from the war years in a cabinet by the door. My brain sets to work, and I quickly conclude that I need to remove it. "It's amazing how dust can get everywhere," I say, opening the cabinet and discreetly removing the old book. I slip it into the desk drawer in the hall and set to work preparing the food in advance for this evening's dinner.

"It's a shame Adam and his delightful family couldn't join us this evening," Hanna says later as I remove her plate.

"Yes," I say, "but the girls need an early night; it's back to school in the morning."

"True, and we are leaving after breakfast tomorrow. I have to get back to work. I'm not driving this distance next time; we'll fly down," Angela suggests.

"Yes, it's a shame we couldn't have delayed our visit by a few days to be here for the actual anniversary, but never mind; at least we've been. I think Adam ought to visit us in Germany next time, dear," Hanna replies to Angela.

Later, I lay in bed thinking about today's events and suddenly remember the book I hid in the hall. The house is silent, so I creep downstairs to retrieve it, and get fresh ice for my lukewarm water. Back in bed, I open the book and thumb through the pages until I get to August 1944.

22nd August 1944

The enemy has finally retreated after long years of misery, but I feel unable to celebrate the long-awaited liberation after the dreadful events of last night, when I witnessed a vile act in the grounds of the Chateau that I was powerless to prevent. It was a personal vendetta and not necessary for the war effort. As if we haven't suffered enough death and destruction. The overly used saying 'All's fair in love and war.' holds no belief for me, even though I believe a new life will come from it.

I drop the book into my lap, possibly giving poor Noah a headache. Did this man witness the murder of Hans? And, who else knows? The penny slowly drops. Xavier and Alice will be acquainted with the family of these people, or worse, was Alice's father involved? Is that why she's been acting out of character, and Xavier's been absent? Someone dug the hasty gravesite. Did the old General know? There must have been a gunshot, though at that time it perhaps wasn't an unusual sound. Oh, my God. What should I do with this information? Is it evidence? Or am I putting two and two together and coming up with five? The journal doesn't name anyone. What purpose would it serve if the murderer's identity now came to light anyway? They're all dead themselves. My gran used to say, "Let sleeping dogs lie." I spend what's left of the night dozing but not sleeping very much at all.

29

I somehow manage to struggle through breakfast and check-out my guests while pasting a smile on my face. How can I contain this information? Am I committing a crime by withholding it? I've asked myself the same question over and over but don't seem able to reach a satisfactory conclusion. I re-read Father Flory's diary entry, searching between the lines for more information, but the facts are scant. All that I can deduce is that he witnessed a vile act in the grounds of the Chateau, which was a personal vendetta, and a new life will come from it. Besides, of course, the date, which is spot on. What about Alice and Xavier? They allegedly know something, should I confront them? I spend the day deep in thought as I service the guest rooms and go about my usual jobs.

Xavier arrives late afternoon, after catching up with his work on the estate. He asks, "'Ow did it go wiz your German guests?"

"It went well, they were very nice people, but your mother was acting rather strange."

Cautiously raising his eyes to meet mine, he asks, "Strange, in what way?"

"Erm, just a little frosty, and she seemed to avoid Hanna and Angela for some reason."

"Oh, don't worry about zat; she is tired. 'Ow is my son?" He says, changing the subject then moving closer to put his hand on my abdomen.

"Oh, Noah's asleep now I—"

Horrified, Xavier interrupts, "What did you call 'im?"

"Noah," I repeat, unable to help myself.

"Yes, I zought you did." Xavier shakes his head, then says forcefully, "You can't call 'im zat!"

"Why?" I reply, knowing full well that I have a battle on my hands.

"'E needs a good French name—"

"Like Pierre?" I interject.

"Zat's more like it! I wondered if you were joking when you said Noah," he replies, running his hand through his hair as he often does when he's frustrated or worried.

I can't resist winding him up as I give him my well-planned reply, "Well, actually, I wasn't, and I think Noah Pierre Mackley-Besnard is a fine name."

"No, wait a minute. 'E will be a Besnard, not Mackley, and both of zem is too much of a mouthful. 'E is a French baby." Xavier is determined to win me over.

"Technically he will be dual nationality, and his name needs to reflect that," I say, starting to feel irritated with him.

Xavier takes my hand and places it to his lips, "Laura, let's not argue, it's not like you. Are you not feeling well?"

"I'm sorry. I'm tired, hot, and grumpy. I didn't get much sleep last night. Did you have a good weekend with Gus?" I ask, deciding to change the subject. It's not Xavier's fault that someone was murdered on my land seventy-five years ago; he wasn't even born.

Three in the morning rolls around, and I'm still wide-awake mulling over some of my problems. What should we call Noah? We need to decide on a surname, as well as his first name! Then there's the gold. I must sell it to pay for the attic. I'll get in touch with Leo. And what about Hans? Do Xavier and Alice know who killed him, and who can I ask without causing suspicion in the community? I sit bolt upright as an idea comes to me. Henri, the goat man. He was a young boy during the war, but he seems quite knowledgeable of past events, even though he is forgetful of current ones.

Immediately after breakfast, I send Leo an e-mail and tick that job off my long list. I can't do much about Noah's name, not until Xavier is prepared to compromise, so that's a battle for another day. Henri is my next job. I ring his landline, but he doesn't answer. I know he's quite deaf and spends most of his days outside, so I pack some of our home-made produce into a cold bag and set off for the drive into the hills. The significance of the date, the 22nd of August is not lost on me; seventy-five years to the day!

It's unbearably warm, and I'm glad of the air conditioning in my Yeti. The countryside has taken on the arid brown colours that it wore when I first arrived. The sunflowers are also getting to the end of their season. Their drooping brown heads due to harvest soon. How very different this summer is to my last one. I was floundering, out of my depth a year ago, not knowing who I could trust. Monsieur Bertrand, my solicitor, had welcomed me to the Chateau, then gone off the very next day for a whole month, leaving me to fend for myself. The journey to Henri's passes by while I smile to myself, remembering the ups and downs of the last twelve months.

I arrive to find no sign of life. Gone are the bleating goats and their kids, with no sign of Henri. What's happened? I bang on his peeling front door but get no response. Next, I try to peer through his small window, wiping away the dirty film that has settled with my hand. There's no movement inside. A middle-aged woman wearing a pale blue tunic appears from around the corner of the house. "Bonjour, can I help you?"

"Oh, hello," I say. "I'm looking for Henri. Do you know where he is?"

"Yes, in bed. Who are you?"

"I'm Laura, his friend. He sold me some goats in the spring. Is he ill?"

"Sorry, I'm his nurse, and I cannot discuss his condition with you, but if you wait a minute, I will ask him if he wants to see you." She heads into the house. I stand in his little garden and wonder what happened to his beloved goats. The woman returns. "You may enter," she says, opening the door wide for me.

"Oh Henri, what's the matter?" I ask, kneeling beside his bed in the dreary parlour.

Henri lifts his head and places his fragile hand in mine. "I'm tired," he says with a raspy voice, then proceeds to cough violently.

"Poor Henri, is there anything I can do for you?" I ask. "I've brought lunch; chevre and cherry milkshake, made with goat's milk," I add.

His nurse produces a straw and helps him to sip the cold, sweet liquid. After a few mouthfuls, he waves it away, closes his clouded eyes and rests his head back on the mountain of pillows his nurse has placed behind him. "It's good to see you again, Laura. How are the goats?" He whispers. I take his cold hand and proceed to tell him about the new kids and chat about life back at the Chateau. I also mention the finding of the body of the German soldier. "Nasty business that was," he says, opening his eyes to look at me.

"What, Henri?"

"The body of the German. I've forgotten his name."

"He was called Hans, but how do you know of him?"

"Yes, Hans. I remember now. He was a good man, really. Shame he was on the wrong side. Well, that's what my mother said at the time," he replies, plainly struggling for breath.

"I'm tiring you, Henri. You need to rest. I'll come back another day."

He sinks back into the pillows once more and remains silent, falling asleep immediately, so I go in search of his nurse, who is hanging washing in the garden. I ask, "How long has he been like this?"

"A few weeks, but he's deteriorating," she says. "If you want to know any more, you must speak to his son, but he hardly ever visits. I'm leaving soon. Lock the door behind you and put the key under the milk churn by the door."

After the nurse has left, I go back inside the dark house. The kitchen consists of a worn stone sink, with an ancient geyser above, a scrubbed pine table and an oven that wouldn't look out of place in a museum. I hear Henri coughing and hacking and rush to his side. Once his cough subsides, he seems confused and asks, "Hello, when did you get here?"

"I've been here a while," I say. "You were telling me the story of the German soldier at the Chateau."

Recognition dawns on his face, then a frown creases his brow, "Yes, a nasty business that was," he repeats.

"How did you know about him, Henri?"

"My father. He was a member of the resistance. I used to help them, you know…" he trails off as another coughing fit follows. I feel guilty for encouraging him to talk, but I need to know. His breathing slows to a steady rhythm, and just as I think he's asleep, he opens his eyes and continues, saying, "Where was I?"

"Your father was in the resistance and knew of Hans," I offer in the way of assistance.

"Yes, that's it. Father was in the valley that night, trying to make the German retreat as difficult as possible, and liberating the items they had left behind when he heard the shot. He went to the Chateau but only found the priest and estate manager digging a grave." Henri's breathing once more becomes erratic as his small body is sent into spasm by more coughing. I watch, powerless to help this poor man, waiting for the episode to pass. After another short nap, he registers my presence with a weak smile.

"Do you know who shot him?" I ask.

Henri looks at me in confusion then says, "Shot who?"

"Hans, the German officer, Henri; the one killed at the Chateau." I remind him. Unfortunately, his mind goes elsewhere.

"My son has sold my goats," he says, looking at me with a pained expression.

I put my hand on his bony shoulder in sympathy. Another coughing fit ensues, and I place the straw between his thin blue lips once it ends. "Could I have your son's telephone number, Henri, so that I can enquire about you?" He nods slightly then closes his eyes as exhaustion takes over. I find the number next to the old phone, jot down his son's details and leave, not wishing to cause him further stress. I lock the door as instructed, and I climb back into my Yeti, grateful of its comforts, and drive home with a heavy heart, knowing I'll not see poor Henri again.

Later, I run through Henri's words in my head. Father Flory and the estate manager dug the grave; that must have been Xavier's grandfather, Pierre. Alice's father. Henri didn't say that Pierre fired the shot or had any other role other than digging the grave with Father Flory. So, he's probably innocent. Henri, in fact, didn't tell me who killed Hans. Perhaps he didn't know. Father Flory wrote that it was a personal vendetta, so it must have been a member of Adam's family that killed him; mustn't it? Xavier's father would probably be considered an accessory to murder, though, having hidden the body with the priest. What a mess. I spend yet another unsettled night mulling over the facts. I know Xavier's grandfather was involved; that's if I can believe what Henri said. Does anyone else know apart from Xavier and Alice? I doubt it. Most of the stories and secrets are lost, along with the people who kept them. And, this is now my secret to keep. Should I document what I know? Probably. One day I may write that book that I promised, to immortalise Henri and others like him.

30

A few days later, I receive an email from Leo with the contact details of a reputable firm who buys and sells gold and other assets. I send them an enquiry and get a response from Monsieur Ardoin, eager to make an appointment to visit me tomorrow. I quickly check that the gold bar is still nestled in my underwear drawer then agree a time — 3.30 pm. Xavier will have left by then if he calls in for lunch. A sense of guilt crashes over me. Xavier and Alice don't know about its existence or the attic conversion. Do I need to tell them? It doesn't take me long to decide that it's genuinely none of their business. They currently only work for me. Yes, I'm carrying Xavier's baby, but we aren't yet officially an item. Sometimes I wonder if we ever will be. And, I now know that they are keeping a massive secret from me too.

Xavier arrives for lunch at 1.20 pm with Gus and the dogs. I prepare them a sandwich and a drink. Gus asks with innocent enthusiasm, "Laura, Dad is taking me swimming to the gorges this afternoon, would you like to come?"

What a tempting offer. There's nothing I'd like better than to float my clammy, swollen body in the fresh, clear water. Truly regretful, I say, "Erm, I'm sorry; another time, perhaps. I'm meeting a potential client this afternoon."

"Who?" Xavier asks curiously, salad leaves hanging from his mouth.

"Oh, a man who emailed looking for a venue for some corporate event; not very exciting but it's business," I reply, wiping my sweaty palms once more on my trousers while trying to sound casual.

"Do you want me to stay?" Xavier asks raising an eyebrow.

"No. Err… no, thank you, it's fine," I say. "You two go and enjoy yourselves. He probably won't stay long anyway. Then I'll try to put my feet up for a while." Feeling irritated, I add, "Another time."

"I'll leave ze dogs wiz you." Xavier smiles. I nod, glad to have their company at least.

Once Xavier and Gus have left, I lock the doors, retrieve the gold bar and take it into the drawing-room, concealing it in the bottom of a large vase, then instruct Beau to sit on duty. I know he will guard it with his life. I position myself on the big window seat and stare down the drive for the next twenty minutes, feeling uncomfortable, until I notice a movement; a large silver car activates the alarm on the gatepost. Is this him? I'm beginning to wonder now if I should have asked Xavier or someone to be here with me. A glance at the oversized clock confirms that it's only five minutes to three, more than half an hour early. Why do I feel so on edge? Beau seems to be able to read my uneasiness and stands to attention, awaiting a command. Freckles' watches him with his head cocked to one side then copies his actions. The car comes to a halt outside and my phone pings with an incoming email.

Mademoiselle Mackley, this is Monsieur Ardoin at your service. I am outside with a colleague. Can we park at the rear of your property?

This situation doesn't feel right. What should I do? Beau now has his teeth bared as a bald man climbs out of the vehicle wearing an ill-fitting suit with a checked shirt, which would look more at home on a lumberjack. Surely this isn't the same firm that Leo recommended. My gut instinct kicks in, and I immediately ring Valentina, but it goes to voicemail. What should I do now? My heart rate spikes and I begin to panic. Noah reacts by giving me a sharp kick in my ribs. Poor Noah. "I'm sorry, baby," I say as I place a hand over my swollen tummy. I know this isn't going to be good for him. Taking a few deep breaths, I attempt to calm myself down, then look back through my recent emails from Leo and click on the link he sent me and ring the number.

"Hello, it's Miss Mackley. I'm ringing to confirm that the person you have sent out to visit me is called Monsieur Ardoin?"

"Hello Miss Mackley, we do indeed have a Monsieur Ardoin working here, but he is on annual leave at the moment. What is the visit in connection with?" The voice on the other end of the line asks. I make my apologies and fob her off with a plausible explanation while continuing to monitor the situation. Moments later the man outside gets back in his car and drives around to the rear of the Chateau. Think, Laura, think. Banging on the back door follows shortly, which sets Beau and Freckles off into a frenzy of vicious barking. Should I let them out to deal with this man? I don't want to involve the police. Running through the possible scenarios in my head, I decided against letting the dogs out in case they have a gun.

I leave them snarling behind the back door and retrieve the gold bar, taking it swiftly upstairs and placing it back with my underwear. Then look down through a rear window to see the two men standing on the back step. Who are they? I dig into the recesses of my mind and recognition dawns. It's Jake and Pierre, the ghost hunters in disguise. They've both shaved their heads! How dare they! This attempt is their third to penetrate my Chateau. What do they want and how did they find out about my gold? Their banging gets louder, and they begin to shout. I think back to their previous bungled attempts, none of which were very well thought out. They must be working for someone. But whom? Judging by their clothes, it appears that they aren't very successful, and I begin to calm down a little. Nevertheless, I need to get rid of them, and for good this time.

My phone rings. It's Adam.

"Hi Laura," he says. "I'm free this afternoon and thought I'd come over to carry on in the attic if that's okay?"

Relieved, I shout, "Adam! Yes! Yes, please come, right now!"

Concerned, he asks, "Is everything alright?"

"No, Adam, it's not." Panic makes my voice crack, "I've got two men outside being a nuisance; they've been before, and I can't get rid of them."

"I'm on my way, stay on the line…" he says as I hear his engine rev. I go up into the attic and watch from the balcony, willing Adam's van to come into sight while I listen to the dogs barking and the two suspects shouting. It feels like an eternity but eventually, the familiar van turns into the drive and I tentatively creep downstairs, armed with my brass candlestick. Hurriedly, I let Adam in through the front door. He's carrying a vicious looking pick.

"Where are they?" He grunts. He then looks at me and asks, "Are you okay?"

"Yes, yes," I say, waving away his concern. "They're at the back door…" Adam strides swiftly through the kitchen with his weapon raised in anger. "Adam, they might be armed," I shout behind him as he enters the porch. The reprobates frantically scramble back into their car as Adam begins to unlock the door and releases the agitated dogs outside. "Stop Adam, let them go!" Adam turns to look at me, with anger and frustration plastered across his face. Then the adrenaline leaves my body, and I begin to shake uncontrollably as the tears start falling.

"Oh Laura, ring the police," he says, his features now softening. I shake my head vehemently. Putting his weapon down, he approaches me, clearly unsure of what to do next and says, "Shall I call the doctor or Xavier?"

"No, no. I'll be okay," I sob. "They've gone now," I say, wiping away the tears as the car fishtails down the side of the Chateau and up the drive.

31

Adam pours me a cold drink and insists that I lay down while I recount the story of the ghost hunters. I lay on the couch in the drawing-room, Adam places the glass on the coffee table and asks, "What do you think they're after?"

"Anything they can get, they're con-men — opportunists. Please don't say anything to Xavier; he'll only worry—"

Adam interrupts, "You can't just pretend it didn't happen…"

"I know, I'll think of something; someone must know who they are."

He eventually leaves me to rest and busies himself in the attic. I pour some lavender oil into a burner and slowly drift off to sleep with three dogs at my side. My phone wakes me. It's Valentina. She says, "Sorry, I missed your call. How are you?" She spends the next five minutes listening as I emotionally relay my three encounters with my criminal stalkers. Alarmed, she asks, "What does Xavier think about the situation?"

"He doesn't know about this afternoon. He's out with Gus. Please don't tell him; you know what he's like, he'll go after them with his gun, and that won't end well."

"Have you rung the police?"

"They came out last time but couldn't find any fingerprints. They appeared disinterested, despite me showing them the images of the two men."

"Hmm, well, somehow the two men knew that you'd received an email from Leo about the gold. That means either yours or Leo's security is an issue. I very much doubt it will be Leo's. I'm going to call him now. I'll ring you right back," she says, ending the call. Five minutes later she rings back, "I'm sending two men out to see you, our IT man Robert, and the private investigator that we use, Franco; they'll be with you before dark."

"I, erm, I can't…" I stutter.

"Don't worry about the cost. It's as much our problem as yours. Leo will want these men stopped before they can do any more damage."

"Are you coming with them?"

"Sorry, I'm at a function this evening, but Franco and Robert will stay over; if that's convenient? They will be very discreet. You can trust them."

"Yes. Yes, thank you, I'd appreciate that. I'm sorry…"

"Don't be, it's not your fault; we'll get them."

Valentina ends the call, and I reassure Adam that I have back-up coming, then send Xavier a text, informing him that I have two guests, businessmen arriving last minute, hoping that he won't call in. I hear the thud of their helicopter about an hour later before I see it dropping out of the sky onto the front lawn, causing the sides of the large marquee to flap. Two men jump out while the blades are still rotating and, with their heads down, make their way over. Once they reach the gravelled drive, I feel safe and open the door, introducing myself.

They take their bags upstairs, then accept a cold beer and sandwiches. I answer Franco's numerous questions, and he prints out an image of the two men while Robert sets to work with my laptop and tablet. "I'm going to take the dogs out into the yard before I go to bed," I say. It's only 8.30 pm, but I'm tired. Franco jumps up and accompanies me, staying a few feet away while I stand in the yard, glad of his company.

After an early breakfast the next morning, Franco suggests, "You should have a safe fitted or take your valuables to a secure location. Have you considered employing a security firm?"

"I've decided to take the gold into town today to try and sell it. There's not much else of value left," I say, trying to think of anything else that may interest a couple of crooks.

"I think you would be surprised, some of these antiques are very desirable; the chandeliers' alone must be worth a fortune. You are vulnerable, living alone." I smile graciously as the helicopter returns, and the pair leave as quickly and efficiently as they arrived, promising to keep me informed.

"Who are zey?" A familiar voice asks as Xavier enters the back door.

"Oh," I say as airily as I can, "two businessmen in the area needing accommodation; acquaintances of Leo and Valentina."

"'umph, 'ow ze ozer 'alf live," he comments, rolling his eyes.

"They seemed pleasant enough," I reply noncommittally. To deflect the conversation and stop Xavier prying further, I ask, "Did you have a good afternoon off with Gus?" With the businessmen easily forgotten; he happily tells me about their trip out. "What are your plans for today?" I add after listening to him.

"Lots to get on wiz…" he continues talking, but a text from Valentina attracts my attention.

I'm sending a car, and it will be with you in an hour.
I've made you an appointment with Monsieur
Ardoin's colleague.

I focus back on Xavier when he asks
brusquely, "Well?"

"Sorry, Xavier," I say apologetically, "well
what?"

"What are you doing today?"

"Oh, I'm going into town to meet Valentina,
she's sending a car in an hour."

"Why doesn't she come 'ere?"

Thinking quickly, I say, "She's passing
through on business and meeting me for
coffee; it will be nice to get out. I'd thought
about looking at strollers and other equipment
while I'm out. I'll ask her which brands Leo
and his wife recommend—"

"Oh," he interrupts, looking disappointed.
"When is your next appointment wiz ze
doctor?"

"I don't need to see the doctor for a while, but I've got an appointment with the midwife next week; would you like to come?" My offer seems to appease him, and his smile returns as he nods and leaves.

An hour later, a car approaches with blacked-out windows. A uniformed man exits and rings the doorbell. "Miss Mackley, I'm here to take you to your appointment," he says, showing me his identification papers. He then assists me into the cool interior. I tightly hold on to my bag containing its valuable cargo. Sitting back into the plush leather, I try to release the tension in my neck and shoulders that seems to accompany me on most days recently. I must try to relax, and it can't be good for Noah. However, I seem to have so many issues to resolve, especially my relationship with Xavier, which appears to have waned recently. Is it him or me? The car glides effortlessly along, taking the miles and the heat in its stride; how can I emulate it?

The driver escorts me into my appointment and insists on sitting in the waiting room while I conduct my business. I'm met in the reception by a man dressed impeccably in a tailored suit. He introduces himself, "Miss Mackley, I'm Monsieur Roux." He escorts me into an office in the back of the building and shuts the door. He continues, "I'm sorry to hear about your distressing experience. I hope you had a pleasant journey."

I make a small noncommittal noise in reply, then say, "Thank you for seeing me at such short notice," as I sit down, placing the offending object on his desk. It's still nestled in its fluffy, pink sock. "I'll be relieved to unburden myself of this weighty cargo," I sigh.

Monsieur Roux looks at me with a fatherly smile on his face, saying, "Well, that's a novel idea; may I?" I lean forward and take it out of the sock and slide it across the deep, purple cloth spread before me.

He opens a desk drawer and takes out a pair of white cotton gloves, pulling them on before replacing his spectacles, which were sitting on his desk, then picks up the bar and positions it on a small weighing scale. Next, he looks on his tablet before lifting his eyes. In full professional mode, he says, "Miss Mackley, I'm pleased to be able to offer you thirty-seven thousand, four hundred Euros and sixty-three cents today." He then sits back and removes his gloves and spectacles, looking at me expectantly. Noah reacts before I do, practising his martial arts and causing me to wince and place my hand over my protruding belly.

Concern flashes across Monsieur Roux's face. "Are you okay, my dear?" He asks. "Would you like a drink of water?" I nod, and he picks up his phone, requesting refreshments. A short time later, I sip the cold water, trying to interpret Noah's reaction. Was he suggesting I break the man's arm off and accept his offer, or was he trying to tell me to fight for more?

My rational thoughts gradually return, and I finally conclude that he was only reacting to my spike of adrenaline and increased anxiety levels. I need to find a way to relax, and alcohol and the hot tub are off-limits for a while. Divesting myself of this particular item will certainly help. Decision made.

"Yes, thank you," I say. "I accept your offer, Monsieur Roux." Fifteen minutes later, I leave my appointment feeling lighter and somewhat wealthier.

32

When I arrive back at the Chateau I'm famished, having missed lunch, and treat myself to a feast, starting with the French onion tart, oozing with chevre. Thinking about goats' cheese makes me remember poor

Henri. How could I have forgotten him? I quickly locate his son's number and press call.

"Hello," I say, "I'm Laura, a friend of your father. I know he's been unwell and I'm enquiring after his health."

"Hello Laura," he says, "the nurse left me a note saying that you had visited, thank you. I'm sorry to inform you he passed away two days ago…" After he finishes speaking, I offer my condolences then end the call feeling hollow. Could I have done more?

Xavier appears from nowhere as I stare down at my oversized slice of French onion tart. My appetite has now gone. "'Ow was your lunch?" he asks quizzically.

"Oh, spoilt," I sigh sadly, "I received a message informing me that Henri had passed away and I didn't feel much like eating. I decided I'd try again, for Noah's sake."

"'Is name isn't Noah," Xavier says, looking at me warily. He closes the distance between us and gently places his hand on my shoulder before continuing, "I'm sorry about Henri. 'E was a good man, but very old. It was inevitable."

I nod. "Yes, I accept it's one of the many things we need to discuss…"

"Ze ozers being?"

I hesitate and look up into his beloved features before continuing, "Lots of things, Xavier. The baby, our future, and we don't seem to be very close anymore…"

"I 'ave tried," Xavier explains, "but you push me away. I feel like you don't want my company anymore. I'm giving you ze space you requested; ze baby will be 'ere in ten weeks, yes?"

I sigh and look away. "Are you genuinely giving me space or avoiding me?" I ask. "Both you and Alice have been different with me since we found out about Hans's murder." He paces the kitchen, running his hands through his long curly hair; a sure sign that he is troubled. I continue, "I think you know more than you're telling me." There. I've said it now. It's out in the open.

He stops pacing and turns to face me, opens his mouth as if to speak, then thinks better of it and continues his march across the kitchen floor. I stand and quietly make my way to the library, returning a moment later with Father Flory's memoirs. Xavier turns once again to look at me with a confused expression as I thumb my way through the book, finding the entry that I suspect refers to the murder. "Does it have something to do with this event?" I ask, passing the book to him. He stills, takes it from me with a frown then pulls out a chair and sits down to read.

22nd August 1944

The enemy has finally retreated after long years of misery, but I feel unable to celebrate the long-awaited liberation after the dreadful events of last night, when I witnessed a vile act in the grounds of the Chateau that

I was powerless to prevent. It was a personal vendetta and not necessary for the war effort. As if we haven't suffered enough death and destruction. The overly used saying 'All's fair in love and war.' holds no belief for me, even though I believe a new life will come from it.

"It gives no names," he says abruptly.

"Thankfully, it doesn't, but I'm convinced it's referring to the night that someone shot Hans Weber. What are you hiding from me?"

"Nozing. I'm 'iding nozing. 'Ow can I be? Mama wasn't even born."

I walk over and place my hand on his shoulder and sit beside him, saying, "Xavier, I'm not blaming you or Alice for anything, but I think you know more than you're saying."

"Who 'as seen zis."

"No one, and as you pointed out, it mentions no names; just a date, which fits."

He walks over to the fridge and pulls out a jug of iced water, pouring us both a glass then placing it on the table and sits back down. He says, "Mama asked me to tell no one, but…" his voice trails off, as if gathering his thoughts, then continues, "…but when I was a child, I was always told not to play by ze bank where we found ze body. Mama was anxious when she realised zere was to be groundworks in zat area. She asked me to try to put ze work off, but I didn't believe her tale. Zat was until we found Hans." He pauses and sits back, and I think this is all I'm going to get; at least it's a start. I open my mouth to speak, but he holds up his hand to silence me and carries on, "She said when she was a little girl, Mama heard her fazer discussing ze events of zat night wiz Aunt Mary; she wanted ze body moving off ze estate, but my grandfazer refused to 'elp."

"Does Alice know who shot Hans?"

"No, of course not," he snaps, "zat is all she knows, and I wish she hadn't over 'eard ze conversation at all!"

I scoot my chair closer and take his hand. "I'm sorry, Xavier…" I trail off, not sure what else to say.

"Don't be, it's not your fault," he says, "just a set of unfortunate circumstances zat we 'ave become mixed up wiz. I zink we need to forget it and move on. Hans 'as gone now and is back wiz 'is family."

I nod. "Yes, I won't mention it to Alice; let sleeping dogs lie," I say.

Cocking his head to one side, he asks, "What 'as zis got to do wiz ze dogs?"

I laugh and explain Gran's old saying to him while I tuck into my tart — my appetite seems to have returned. Once I've finished, I lean back in my chair and say, "Thank you for telling me; now it's my turn to share."

"Share what? I 'ave just eaten 'alf of your lunch." Xavier points out.

I smile then say, "Share my secret. I didn't meet Valentina this morning. I had an appointment…"

Panic and worry flash in Xavier's eyes. He quickly interrupts, "Wiz ze 'ospital? Is ze baby okay?"

"The baby is fine Xavier," I say soothingly. "No, I had an appointment with a company that buys gold." His eyes find mine in surprise, and I continue, "A while ago now, I found a gold bar hidden behind an old skirting board in the attic…" He listens with his mouth wide open as I share my convoluted story, including my unfortunate visit from the conmen, Jake and Pierre. He listens patiently, not once interrupting until I've finished.

"Sapristi!" He says, leaning back wide-eyed, "Why didn't you tell me?"

"Oh, lots of reasons."

"What reasons?" He demands.

"Well, first of all, I didn't want you going after them with your gun; who knows how that would have ended?" Xavier tries to interrupt, but I put my hand up to silence him and continue, "Also, I didn't want you to know about the attic…"

"What about ze attic?"

It's now, or never, so I take a deep breath and say, "I've decided to convert it into an apartment so we, err, I can live up there with the baby."

His eyes find mine and the expression in them softens. I hope he's missed my slip of the tongue, but I doubt it. He reaches out his hand and takes mine in his before saying, "Zank you for telling me. When will it be finished?"

"Oh, it won't be ready until next year; there's no rush. Adam is doing it in-between jobs when the weather prevents him from doing outside work. It's cheaper that way." I shrug.

"I can 'elp—"

"Xavier," I interrupt, "you have enough to do on the estate just now, and Gus needs you. I'm going to see the midwife in the village tomorrow, are you still coming with me?" I ask, trying to distract him.

His face lights up, and he says, "Yes. Yes, please. What time?"

"Eleven in the morning."

"I'll be 'ere," he says, then looks into my eyes and adds, "but promise me if you 'ave any more problems, you will ring me immediately."

I nod instantly and say, "I promise, but surely, we've had enough problems to last a lifetime!"

Xavier shrugs and turns to leave with Beau following, but he stops and instructs his faithful companion to stay. "I am leaving Beau wiz you until we deal wiz zose two men. Lock ze door behind me." I don't argue as I watch him close the door and leave. Despite the intense heat outside, the kitchen suddenly feels cold and empty without him.

33

Despite feeling better for having had a heart to heart with Xavier, I still spend the night tossing and turning and visiting the toilet several times. Surely Noah has no more room in there! I stack my pillows into an armchair shape behind me and give up on the idea of sleep; sore breasts, aching legs and an itching abdomen get the better of me, so I reward myself with a peek at my favourite website. Thirty weeks. Noah is the size of a cabbage and can hear and see. Allegedly, if I place a bright light on my belly, he should turn his head to face it. I reach over to my bedside table and grab my torch and have a go; a few seconds later, I get a boot in the ribs. It seems

Noah doesn't like being disturbed in the night either. Let's hope he remembers that once he's born!

Oh, I should start buying essential baby items now. Alice still has a case full of baby clothes that were Gus's beside the knitted cardigans she's been busy making. I don't know how she finds the time. I attended several baby showers back in England, but I've no intention of arranging such an event. The locals would think I'd lost my marbles! I do, however, need a new car seat and cot. I ought to look at feeding equipment too, in case I struggle to breastfeed. I trawl through various websites for information, but exhaustion gets the better of me, and I eventually fall asleep.

I'm in the walled garden picking fruit. I can see a juicy peach just out of reach. I stretch further than I should, and my waters break; it starts with a small trickle but quickly picks up into a torrent, and I'm carried away by the volume down the stream into the pond which is now flooding over the sluice gate.

"Help! Xavier, help!" My shouting wakes me with a jump and Noah responds by energetically kicking. I try to calm my breathing as I look around and instinctively feel my nightdress and bedding. It's dry. Another weird dream! I need to relax, but how? Perhaps I'd feel calmer if I were better prepared? I'll sort out antenatal classes and order some essentials online, but first, breakfast. I'm famished.

I'm browsing on the internet when Xavier enters the kitchen. "What are you looking at?" Xavier asks.

"Oh, all the items I need to purchase for Noah, erm, the bump," I say, and he smiles as he fills the kettle with water and spoons coffee into the cafetière. "Tea for me please, or I'll not make it to the village without squatting down behind a bush."

Placing the mugs on the table, he puts his hand over mine and looks at my screen, doing a double-take. "Err," he says, "what are zose?"

"Erm," I say, wriggling in my seat, uncomfortable and slightly embarrassed, "nipple shields…"

"Really!" Xavier exclaims, then frowns in confusion. "Why do you need zem? I'm sure ze ancestors managed wizout such zings."

"Yes, they had no choice, it's called progress; I'll only order one pack. Oh, what size?" I mumble, which has the effect of causing Xavier to burst into a fit of laughter, something I've rarely witnessed, and I can't help but join in. Unexpectedly, a sharp pain grabs me. "Ouch!" I cry, putting my hand on my now tight abdomen.

Instantly sober, Xavier asks as he kneels beside me, "Laura, what's wrong?"

I take a few deep breaths, and the sensation begins to ease. "Erm, I think that was what they call a Braxton Hicks," I explain. "It's a type of practice contraction. It's normal, but not pleasant."

"We need to tell ze midwife. Come on, let's go," he says, looking worried.

Yvette is once again behind the reception desk when we arrive at the doctor's office. "Hello, Miss Mackley," she says, "you're early."

"Yes," Xavier says. "She 'ad a strange contraction; we need to see ze midwife…"

"Oh dear, I'll see if she's free," Yvette replies.

We're shown into a small room by a young woman that I haven't previously met. "Hello," she says. "I'm covering for my colleague who's on holiday; what appears to be the problem?"

"She 'as ze contraction—" Xavier began.

I interrupt by saying, "I'm sorry to trouble you. I think it was probably a Braxton Hicks contraction. It took me by surprise; it was quite uncomfortable."

"Yes, they can be, how many weeks along are you?"

"Zirty," Xavier interrupts.

I look back at the midwife apologetically, she then asks me to lie on the couch and begins palpitating my abdomen. She says, "Everything feels okay. I'll check the heartbeat next." She then attaches a baby heart monitor. The room soon fills with the reassuring sound of Noah's heart beating steadily and strongly. Xavier visibly relaxes and leans back in his chair, smiling. "All appears to be fine with the baby," the midwife says. "You, on the other hand, seem rather tense; you need to relax a little."

"Yes, I do feel rather wound up at times; it's difficult when you can't have a glass of wine or a soak in the hot tub."

"Mm, how about a massage? That would help you to relax," the midwife says.

"But where? Do you do that here?" I ask.

"No, you would have to drive to town I'm afraid…"

"I can do zat," Xavier announces, grinning.

"There you are, problem solved," she says with a smile and gives me a leaflet suggesting some essential oils that are safe for use in pregnancy. A glance at the list confirms what I already know. Lavender and chamomile; both of which I already possess.

"Okay, where are ze oils?" Xavier asks as we enter the Chateau.

"It's very kind of you to offer but…"

"No but's, you need to relax."

"Thank you, but it's too early; I'll be asleep all afternoon then I won't sleep tonight."

"Okay," he says. "I'll come back about eight, zen you will sleep all night, yes?" He then picks up the list of baby items that I've left beside my laptop and reads it slowly. Xavier then looks up. "On Saturday, I will take you shopping for some of zeese. You might feel better zen," he adds before leaving me alone once more with my thoughts.

I know he's a good man, but there has been no mention of the future. Does he even want to move in with me when Adam finishes the attic? And what about Alice? We can't leave her alone at the farmhouse. The only way I'm going to be able to relax is by solving some of these issues. And, the baby's name; what on earth are we going to call him? I spend the rest of the afternoon attending to my jobs, deep in thought. The only thing that seems clear about our future is the lack of clarity.

34

After supper, my phone rings — an unknown number. Should I answer it? Curiosity gets the better of me. After all, it might be business. "Hello?" I say.

"Miss Mackley, sorry to bother you. It's Marco, the private investigator."

"Oh, Marco, hello. Thank you for calling. Have you found them?"

"Unfortunately, I haven't been able to locate the two men in question; they appear to have several identities…"

"Oh dear. That's disappointing."

"Yes, I'm sorry, it is. The duo have, however, left a digital trail which links them to a company in Paris," he gives me the name then continues, "does that mean anything to you?"

I rack my brain but can think of nothing, "No, sorry. I've never heard of that company."

"Okay, not to worry; we'll keep searching. If you remember anything, call me on this number." I end the call and stare at my phone.

"Who was zat?" Xavier asks as he once again appears in the kitchen.

"Oh, just Marco, the detective keeping me posted; they've found a lead in Paris of all places."

"Do you know anyone in Paris?"

"No. No, I don't think I do. What do these people want with me?"

He steps forward and takes my phone from me, putting it on silent. He places it on the table then takes my hand, gently pulling me from my chair. "Where are we doing ze massage?"

"Oh, erm, I'd forgotten about that…" I say, retrieving my hand from his.

"Well, I 'aven't; let's go upstairs," he says, turning to lock the back door then shepherding me towards the hall. Once in my bedroom, he positions a chair to face me and arranges a pillow to cover the back, then produces a small bottle of almond oil, pouring it into a teacup he'd filched from the kitchen.

"Where did you get that?"

"Mama uses it for cakes, I've looked on ze internet; it's ze correct oil, and safe for ze baby…"

It's now or never, "Yes, about the baby — he needs a name."

"Not now, you need to relax," he begins mixing a drop of lavender and chamomile into the small cup of almond oil. "Now, take off your shirt and sit ze wrong way around on ze chair, leaning your head on ze pillow."

"But how did you know that?" I ask, surprised.

"I did some research; you can't exactly lay on your tummy, you would squash ze baby."

I pull my oversized blouse over my head and sit as instructed, letting my shoulders flop forwards and gently rest my cheek on the soft pillow.

"May I?" He asks, touching the clasp on the back of my bra.

"Mm," I respond into the pillow. Xavier unclips my bra, taking the pressure off my swollen breasts, then rubs some oil onto his hands to warm it and gently spreads the heated oil over my shoulders and down my back. My body sags forward as I let out a deep sigh. "Mmm," I groan, "that's amazing, thank you."

"Shh, close your eyes and relax."

I do as instructed, and enjoy the experience as he places gentle, feather-like strokes down my back and gradually begins to increase the pressure. His strong hands move effortlessly over my shoulders, up my neck, and down my arms, before gliding down my back and repeating the movement. I don't know how he's doing it. At any one time, it feels like he has at least four hands on my body. My bedroom begins to fill with the sublime aroma of the oil as all of the tension is released from my body. Noah seems to have dropped off to sleep too. The next thing I feel is a gentle tap on my shoulder as he places a towel around me. "'Ow was zat?"

"Oh, Xavier, it was fantastic; I feel so much better. Thank you."

"Zere is some oil left, can I put it on ze bump?" He asks, looking at me cautiously.

I turn and sit the correct way around on the chair and lean back. He looks into my face waiting for permission. I nod, and he pours a generous amount of oil into his cupped hand and gently spreads it on my swollen belly. It feels wonderful. Noah chooses this moment to wake up and kick his father. "Ze baby! I can feel ze baby!" Xavier says excitedly. He then kneels and places a soft kiss where moments before, his son's foot had made contact with him. The whole experience feels surreal, and I can no longer hide my emotions. A solitary tear slides down my cheek. Xavier stands and places an oily kiss in its path, followed by another on the end of my nose. "You are amazing, zank you for 'aving my baby." He puts his arms underneath mine and helps me to stand, guiding me to my bed. "You need to sleep." He pulls the cover down and gestures for me to climb into bed.

"I need to use the bathroom first," I say and head into it. Xavier's busy tidying the chair away when I return. I turn to look at him and say, "Please stay."

"Zere is nozing I would like more, but I will not... err, you know, when you are big wiz ze baby. I will sleep on ze floor."

"No, you won't. Please, hold me." He stills and looks at me, obviously torn, then pulls his clothes off and climbs into bed. I scoot over to him and fall asleep, cradled in his protective arms.

35

When I awake the following morning, I'm alone. The story of my life. Why does everyone leave me? First, my parents, then Gran; followed by several men, including Enzo. Why has Xavier gone? I look around me but can't even find a scribbled note. I rest my head back on my pillow, and the aroma of lavender and chamomile wafts over me. I begin to relax as I remember last night's massage and wonder what the time is. A glance at my phone says it's past 10 am. No wonder Xavier's gone, he's got work to do. An image of him climbing out of bed, and stealthily creeping around trying not to wake me comes to mind, and my feelings of frustration replace with a warm, tingling sensation. Slowly, I waddle over to the window and open the voile curtains. It's another sweltering day. We desperately need some rain. Down in the kitchen, I consume an ample breakfast while listening to the radio; apparently, storms are expected later today — a welcome relief for the parched earth.

After dealing with emails, several bookings and two wedding enquiries, I take the dogs and make my way over to the campsite. I need to warn my guests of the impending storm, especially the ones staying in tents. Xavier, with some help, has erected a simple log cabin, which we've furnished with basic camp beds and emergency rations. Hopefully, the field won't flood again, but I can do very little about the strength of the wind that blows down this valley.

The heat soon gets the better of me, and I return to the cool interior of the Chateau for some much-needed water. Once suitably refreshed, I open the back door to hang my laundry outside. An acrid smell invades my nostrils. Smoke. There must be a fire, but where? I waddle up to the attic as fast as my puffy ankles will carry me and step out onto the balcony. Plumes of thick smoke are rising into the sky off to my left. Thankfully, it looks to be beyond the vineyard, on my neighbour's land. I can hear shouting in the distance and some movement down by our pond. I grab my binoculars from the shelf and squint my eyes to try to block out the glare from the relentless sun. It's Xavier and Gus, they appear to be pumping water out of the pond and spraying it over the perimeter wall into the neighbour's land. I must go and see if I can help.

By the time I arrive, Gus is by himself, wrestling with a long hosepipe and aiming the water over the wall. As I get closer, I ask, "Gus, where's your dad?"

"He's gone next door to help. A hay meadow has set on fire, and the wind is blowing it towards us; we have to stop it reaching the vines," he puffs.

"Here, let me help," I say, trying to take the hose from him.

"No, no, Laura. Papa said you have to stay indoors…"

"I will not stay indoors and watch the estate go up in smoke," I say, then add, "has someone called the fire service?"

Gus looks at me and loses his grip on the hose, spraying water over both of us. He nods and says, "Yes, but they're all out, attending to wildfires."

"Gus, I'll take the hose," I say, trying not to alarm him as embers and small charred remains of vegetation begin to rain down on us. "You can fill those buckets from the pond and start pouring water onto the dead grass on our side of the wall."

He nods and hands me the hosepipe. I begin spraying over the wall once more. I'm startled by a voice behind me and turn to see Pedro and two other men from the village, covered in sweat, and streaked with soot marks. Pedro looks at me solemnly then jumps into the pond and fixes another hose on to the submerged pump and sets about drenching the parched earth on the neighbour's land. The other two men follow on behind, helping Gus with more buckets, but it's a lot of effort for little return.

One of the men from the village shouts, "Feu!"

A small flame has taken hold off to our left. The other man runs over with his fire beater and extinguishes it quickly as Pedro gestures for me to move further down in the direction of the falling debris. Gus stills for a moment, looking exhausted, then picks up his bucket and continues valiantly. I walk as far as the hose will reach and hold on as the water sprays out at a considerable force, but it's not enough. More firebombs rain down on us as the wind whips up into a frenzy. One of them takes hold behind me in the first row of the vines. Gus is onto it with a bucket of water, but it quickly spreads to the next row as the gusting wind assists its advance. I turn my hose onto the area and manage to extinguish it, knocking Gus to the floor and soaking him in the process. He pauses to rest for a moment, and I'm about to rush to his side when one of the men shouts, "Get up, lad, and carry on!" Gus does as he's told with a shrug of his small shoulders, and I can see he is every inch his father's son. Xavier must be so proud of him; I know I am.

Another firebomb contacts the ground, causing a small fire, which quickly takes hold of the dried grass. It begins to spin in the wind as the flames get higher; emulating the dust devils that were dancing there earlier. I tug on the slippery hose with all my might, but it will reach no further. So, I grab a bucket and rush back to the pond, coughing as a wall of dense smoke blows in my direction, obscuring my vision and causing my eyes to sting. Gus appears through the smoke, taking the bucket from me and shouting, "Laura! Think of the baby. Stop and rest."

I know he's right, so I drop to my hands and knees and crawl to a safe distance while I watch the three men and Gus tackle the fires as they break out around them. Glancing down, away from the swirling flames, I witness an army of gigantic ants carrying their larvae in a procession away from danger; protecting the next generation, and I know it's what I must do. I cradle my swollen belly as another Braxton Hicks contraction causes discomfort. Poor Noah, can he feel them too? More fires break out around us, and I'm sure we're not going to win this battle against mother nature. The vines — we're going to lose Xavier's precious vines; he's tended them all of his life.

The dead vegetation on our side of the wall is well and truly alight now, and the beaters are fighting a losing battle. "Go, save yourselves," I try to shout, but my words remain hidden in the crackle of the flames and the rush of the gusting winds. I look up to the sky and begin to pray; not something I've done very often, but it's the last resort. "Please, dear God, please, keep my loved ones safe," I chant.

Xavier, Gus, and Alice, nothing else matters
— the vines, the gnarled olive trees that are at
least a hundred years old, or the Chateau —
these three people are all that matter to me.
And Noah. "I'll call the baby whatever Xavier
chooses if you, please, keep us all safe!" I
shout. I pull myself up and carefully walk
forwards through the choking smoke. I must
take Gus to safety. Pedro comes into view
through the dense blanket of smoke, and he
slowly sinks to his knees as he looks skywards.
The other two men stop beating the flames
and follow suit. "Why have you stopped?" I
croak, taking a hose from one of them.

"Madonna. She 'as answered our prayers," a
familiar voice shouts from over the wall.
Xavier, he's safe. I sag to the floor as I feel the
drops of rain landing on my exhausted body.
It begins as usual, with gentle drumming,
having little impact, but I know that it will
soon be falling from the sky in torrents. I
close my eyes as the raindrops pick up speed
and deliver the lifeline that we desperately

need. An intense flash of lightning swiftly followed by a loud rumble of thunder, and the lifesaving storm has arrived in earnest.

"Laura, it's raining; we're safe," Gus croaks as he crawls over to my side. I wrap my arms around his young body and hold him tight.

"Yes, we're all safe," I say as Noah gives me a boot in the ribs. The rain stings as it hits my skin, but I don't care. My tears join it as they soak the earth, my earth; this small corner of rural France that is now my home.

"Zank God!" My favourite voice says as Xavier sinks to his knees at our side. We sit together and embrace each other as the fires, at last, succumb to the force of nature, and the parched earth refreshes. I stand on shaky legs a little later and survey the damage. Much of the ground lies blackened around us, and the leaves and fruit have withered on the first row of the vines.

Horrified, I say, "I'm sorry..."

Xavier jumps to his feet, cradles me as I begin to wobble, and says, "We need to get you 'ome, where you should 'ave stayed."

"What about the vines?" I ask.

"Zey are of little consequence," he says. "All zat matters are zat you and Gus are safe; and Noah. Come, let's go 'ome."

We turn to head back to the Chateau, through the torrential rain. When we get about halfway we see Alice heading in our direction. "Oh, thank God you are all okay. I came as fast as I could when I heard," Alice shouts through the smoke-filled rain, with Monsieur le Maire close behind her.

"Nana! Nana!" Gus responds, running into her open arms.

36

Back at the Chateau, Alice pours everyone large glasses of iced water. "Drink," she says, "you will be dehydrated."

Monsieur le Maire takes Pedro and his helpers back to the village while Alice runs a cool bath. Xavier helps me to undress and lowers me into the water. "I will never take water for granted, ever again," I say, as I let the precious liquid trickle through my fingers. Xavier picks up a jug and gently pours water over my hair, then begins to massage shampoo into my scalp. "Mm," I moan. Once washed and rinsed, he helps me out and drapes a soft fluffy towel around me, while my mind wanders back to the fire. "Xavier, earlier, when you said that all that mattered to you was that we were safe, you called the baby Noah."

He looks at me and solemnly nods as he strips out of his filthy, tattered clothes, and immerses himself in the soapy water, saying, "Yes, I prayed to Madonna and swore zat I would call ze baby whatever you wanted as long as she kept us all safe."

As the water rolls over his shoulders, he winces. I ask, "What's the matter?" as I walk towards him, grateful for the distraction while trying to hide the intense feelings of love that are welling up inside of me.

He waves me away, saying, "Nozing, it's nozing."

"I'll be the judge of that," I say, then I notice a burn about the size of a fifty-pence-piece that's now blistering on his left shoulder. "I'll soak a dressing in lavender oil and cover it for you when you get out. You need to be careful so that it doesn't get infected."

"I've 'ad much worse zan zis in my time." He quickly rinses his hair and climbs out of the bath, saying, "Bed, you are going to bed for ze rest of ze day."

"What about Gus?"

"Mama has taken 'im 'ome; 'e is going to bed too."

"I'm sorry about the vines…"

"Don't be, zey too 'ave lived zrough worse. Only a few were spoilt, and zey will regrow next year. It could 'ave been worse; far, far, worse."

"Was anyone injured next door?"

"A few minor burns," he admits with his usual shrug, "and some smoke inhalation. Nozing more serious."

"Good," I say and pour a glass of iced water from the jug at my bedside as Xavier gestures once more for me to climb into bed. I hand him the other empty glass. "Your turn, drink," I say sternly before lying on my comfortable bed, letting out a loud groan as my limbs relax. "Lay with me," I say. "You must be exhausted too."

Xavier hesitates then climbs onto the bed beside me and places gentle kisses on my forehead, saying, "Zis is for you and Gus." He moves down and adds, "Zis one is for Noah." His lips graze my abdomen. He is asleep before I've even closed my eyes. I gaze at his relaxed form, and a warm, glowing sensation travels through the length of my body. Noah. He's going to let me call him Noah. I lay for a while, listening to the thunder crashing outside, and I know that I too must compromise. I had my prayers answered also, and with a significant decision made, I close my eyes and succumb to exhaustion. Noah Besnard. He will take his father's surname.

When I awaken, the sky is painted crimson by a stunning sunset. I can't believe I've slept so long. Every inch of my body screams in pain as I waddle downstairs. There's a note on the kitchen table. It says,

Ring when you wake up. X

I pick up the phone and call Xavier. He asks, "Laura, 'ow are you feeling?"

"I'm aching but otherwise okay. How are you and Gus?"

"Good, we are both good. Mama 'as made supper for you, I'm on my way." Xavier ends the call, giving me no opportunity to protest.

I pour two glasses of iced water and watch Beau's ears prick up as he stares at the back door; he knows his master is on his way. I unlock the door and stand outside in my nightdress, admiring my surroundings as I look to the sky. The hairs on the back of my neck stand on end and my skin tingles. I turn around slowly to find Xavier stood in a shaft of evening sunlight, looking at me. "You are truly amazing," he whispers.

"Mm, you don't look too bad yourself," I reply, throwing my arms around his neck. He winces while trying to steady the cold bag in his hand.

"Oh, I'm so sorry; I forgot your burn, let me…"

"I'm okay," he insists, carrying the bag into the kitchen, where he proceeds to unload a small feast onto the kitchen table.

"How many guests are we expecting?" I tease.

"Just ze zree of us."

"Three? Is Gus coming?"

"No, Gus 'as eaten. It's just you, me, and Noah," he says, placing a soft kiss on the end of my nose.

"Are you sure that you want to call him Noah?" I ask. He doesn't speak but offers a subtle nod, so I continue, "Noah Pierre Besnard. I like the sound of that."

His eyes find mine, and a wave of emotion sweeps across his face. He opens his mouth to speak, but nothing comes out. Xavier tries again, and with a wobbly voice repeats, "Noah Pierre Besnard; I like ze sound of zat, too."

"Well," I say, "Noah wants his supper." I tuck into the feast before me. "This is fit for a king. Please thank Alice." After a slice of pie followed by salad and quiche, I begin to slow down, noticing that Xavier hadn't eaten, so I ask, "You haven't had much, aren't you hungry?"

"I ate earlier wiz Gus and Mama."

"But you've worked incredibly hard all day, and you didn't get any lunch because of the fire; have you been back to the vines?"

He lifts his head and nods. "Yes, it looked worse zan it genuinely is; I've pruned ze dead leaves. Zey will come back." A worried expression still lines his face, though.

"Xavier, will you please tell me what's troubling you?"

He leans forward and takes my hand, lifting it to his lips for a kiss, before saying, "You. If anyzing 'ad 'appened to you today…" His words trail off, and he swallows as tears fill his eyes.

I put my spoon down and finish my mouthful of cherry tart, saying, "But it didn't Xavier; I'm still here with your son growing in my belly, feel." I put his hand on my bump. The creases on his forehead smooth as he rests his hand there. I continue, "Xavier, I love you." He opens his mouth once more and closes it while maintaining eye contact. "And I love Gus and Alice too," I say, as tears form in my eyes as well. We gaze at each other in silence, the intensity wrapping us in an intricately woven bubble.

The spell is broken by Freckles scratching on the back door, wanting to be let out. Xavier looks in his direction and then back at me, hesitating, but he chooses to stand and walk over to let the dog out into the yard and follows him. Have I said too much? Doesn't he feel the same way? Isn't this the moment where he should declare his undying love for our son and me? I take a deep breath and stand up, placing the empty plates in the sink then head to the door. "Please thank Alice for supper. Goodnight," I say, closing the door behind him. What just happened?

When all three dogs have had their supper, I waddle back upstairs and lay down on my bed. I can still smell lavender, chamomile, and Xavier on my sheets. Why didn't he tell me that he loves me too? I know he finds it difficult to show emotion, but I had paved the way for him. Perhaps he's tired. Yes, that's it, he must be exhausted after today's events. I'll give him the benefit of my doubt. Minutes turn into hours as I get increasingly frustrated with myself. Should I avoid him for a few days? It's Saturday tomorrow, so it shouldn't be too difficult. He often spends Saturday with Gus.

37

A kiss on my forehead wakes me the next morning. Xavier smiles down at me and says, "Morning sleepy head."

I sit up and look around me. "Xavier, what time is it?"

"After 10 am. Come on, we 'ave shopping to do."

"Shopping? It's Saturday, aren't you doing something with Gus?"

"No, 'e went to a friend's 'ouse for ze day. 'Ave you forgot?"

"Forgot what?"

"Shopping; we are going shopping for zings for ze baby. Yes?" A frown crossing his face, he says, "I know yesterday was crazy, but I zought you would be 'appy."

So much for avoiding Xavier. "Yes, thank you, I had forgotten, and I am happy to be going shopping for the things Noah will need," I say, managing a smile.

Outside, I walk towards my Yeti, but Xavier stops me and says, "I 'ave brought ze truck, we will need it to get ze big items 'ome." He looks at me then continues, "And, yes…" but then stops abruptly and looks at the ground without finishing his sentence.

"Yes, what Xavier?" He sighs and takes my hand, helping me up into his truck. What is it that he wants to say? As I try to get comfortable, I look around in amazement as the aroma of disinfectant makes me sneeze. I exclaim, "You've cleaned it out!" He nods and climbs into the driver's seat and sets off down the drive without looking at me.

He continues driving in silence, and I give up on the idea of having a conversation and look out of the window, watching the village disappear behind us. The countryside flashes by and seems brown and desolate despite yesterday's storm. My mind wanders as an image of the verdant lawn with its precise stripes from my childhood flashed through my mind. My dad was passionate about his garden, what a contrast. I sigh and look back at Xavier, but he continues looking ahead, as though I'm not beside him. What is wrong with him? I can stand the tension no longer and say, "Xavier, I don't know what I've said to upset you, but whatever it was – I'm sorry."

His eyes remain on the road ahead as he abruptly replies, "Nozing. You 'ave said nozing to upset me." Okay, I give up, he'll talk when he's ready. Half-an-hour later, he breaks his silence and looks over at me, his features softening and says, "We're nearly zere." Ten minutes later, we pull into what appears to resemble an industrial estate, and Xavier looks at the directions on his phone. "Somewhere in 'ere is ze baby warehouse," he grumbles.

After taking a few wrong turns, we eventually arrive at a massive rectangular building with a small sign depicting an image of a baby in a stroller. "I didn't know this was here."

"It 'as only been 'ere for a few months, and it's not open to ze public; zey retail to trade only."

"Oh, so we can't go in?"

"Yes, you can, because you 'ave ze 'otel business so you can buy ze baby items for your business. Yes?" He smiles then continues, "Your guests will need ze cot and highchair for ze babies. Yes?"

"Wow, I never thought of that," I say, smiling as he helps me out of his massive truck, and we enter the building. Once passed the reception, we walk into its cavernous interior. It must be the size of a football pitch and stocked floor to ceiling with rows and rows of baby paraphernalia. Cots, strollers, feeding equipment, I don't know where to begin. It's overwhelming.

Sensing my feelings, Xavier takes my hand and asks, "You 'ave ze list?" I fish it out of my bag and hand it to him as he leads me to the far end of the building, saying, "Look, each aisle 'as a label, so we know where to go."

"Erm, I need the toilet first, sorry."

"Okay," Xavier says, following the signs and waits for me outside the restroom. After my comfort break, he asks, "Where do you want to begin?"

"Oh, a cot, I think, but I did rather like the swinging crib that I saw in the department store in town."

"Come," he says, taking my hand once again and leading me down the aisle marked cots and cribs. He produces a tatty piece of paper and a tape measure from his pocket and proceeds to measure some of the mattresses on display. "Which one do you prefer?" He asks, giving me a choice of three different ones.

"Shouldn't we choose a crib first?"

"Erm, no. We only need ze mattress. Now, which one do you prefer?"

"I'm sorry, I don't understand. We need a crib—"

He sighs and turns to me, not letting me finish my sentence, "Trust me, we just need ze mattress." I hesitate, then admit defeat and choose one of the mattresses on display and stand back. Xavier then scans the item with the code reader that we received at the reception, then proceeds to the next aisle, strollers. Xavier admits, "I know nozing about strollers, you choose." I feel a little stunned by the choices and begin the task of trying several out. There are forward-facing, backwards-facing, and removable car seat options, the range is staggering. Twenty minutes later, and I think I've made my choice, a full-size stroller with all-terrain wheels and travel options. It's one of the most expensive but should last until Noah no longer needs it.

Next, on the list, is feeding equipment. As I agonise over the numerous choices, Xavier gets distracted by baby toys. He wanders away and comes back looking pleased with himself as he shows me a soft toy shaped like a tractor. "Erm, I'm not sure that a toy tractor is a priority," I say.

He grins and squeezes the toy, which makes a honking noise. "See, it 'as a loud 'orn; Noah will like it," he then scans the item and returns the toy to its shelf.

"How much does it cost?" I ask.

He looks at me and shrugs. "It doesn't matter. I am buying it for my son."

"Mm," I tease, "I rather think it might be for you." He laughs and shrugs again before continuing down the aisle, "Wait," I say. "I need nipple shields."

"You're on your own wiz zat one," he comments with a chuckle. Next, we arrive in the clothes aisle, and I can't help but notice the pretty, pink selection for girls. I somehow manage to control myself and sigh as I turn around to look at the boy's clothes on the other side of the aisle. They're not nearly as cute. Xavier notices me looking and says, "We don't need ze clothes. Mama 'as saved all of Gus's zings."

"Yes," I sigh, "I have them in a suitcase at home. I'm going to get them washed. But it would have been fun to choose some new ones."

He walks towards me and puts his arm around my shoulder while saying, "When ze baby 'as arrived, we can come back and get some new zings. Besides, people will buy lots, 'e will 'ave more zan 'e can wear. Anyway, 'e is only going to be sick and poop on zem."

An hour later, my stomach reminds me I need to feed myself and my son. I grab Xavier's hand and say, "Come on, I'm famished; I think we have everything on my list, and more besides."

We head to the reception and hand our code reader back to the staff member, who presents Xavier with the bill. "How much is it?" I ask. Xavier shrugs and produces his bank card and pays before I have a chance to gather my thoughts, then we are asked to wait in area D; this feels familiar. "You can't pay for everything," I protest.

"I will do as I please; he is my son."

"Yes, I know, but he's also half mine, you know."

"I will give you ze receipt. It can go zrough ze business…"

We are interrupted by a whiny voice on the announcement system, stating that our order is ready to collect. Xavier locates a large flat trolley and piles the items onto it and pushes it out through the automatic doors. As we walk back to the truck, I say, "Wow, what a lot; I think we got carried away."

Xavier loads the items into the back of his truck then turns and says with a smirk, "I zink ze only unnecessary item is ze nipple shields…"

"Erm," I say, "what about the toy tractor? Anyway, the nipple shields are necessary!"

Xavier shakes his head and helps me back up into the truck, "Food next," he adds and drives back to the village, giving me time to think about our purchases. Why did he want me only to buy a mattress and not a crib? Perhaps he expects Noah to use the one that belonged to Gus? No doubt it was a hand-me-down from someone in the village before that. Well, if it's a tatty mess, I'll order the one that I liked from town.

Xavier carries Noah's equipment up to my bedroom and places the items in a large pile in the corner that is to become the nursery area.

"Zere. Don't lift any of ze heavy boxes—" he admonishes.

"But the stroller needs to be assembled," I interrupt.

"No, zat is staying at ze farmhouse wiz Mama. She insists zat it is bad luck to 'ave it in ze Chateau until ze baby is born."

"That's just an old wives' tale."

"Yes, I agree," he says, shrugging. "But Mama insists. So, we 'ave got everyzing except ze baby now. Yes?"

"Erm, no. I haven't got a crib."

Xavier sighs before saying, "You will 'ave soon." He then says, "I will go check on ze animals now," and heads downstairs.

Once he's gone, I delight in opening the packages and arranging the items in the new chest of drawers and placing the changing equipment on top, along with the toy tractor. I have to admit it is rather cute. Next, I make space in the kitchen for my sterilising unit and feeding paraphernalia. The clothes are next. I empty the suitcase that Alice brought over and go through the items. Some go into charity bags, and I put the rest in to wash. It's hard to imagine that it will be the middle of winter in a couple of months when Noah is born. A flashback of the deep snow that fell last December enters my head. Oh, no! What if I can't get to the hospital? My breathing accelerates, and my heart rate picks up, this has the effect of rousing Noah, who starts to kick. I must try to calm down. I find my bottle of lavender oil and put a few drops onto a tissue and practice my breathing exercise; this seems to help, and Noah soon settles. Once I complete everything I need to do, I sit in the shade with a glass of iced water and prepare a list of questions for the appointment with the midwife next week. The first question is: What happens if the snow is too deep to get to the hospital? My meetings with her are now every two weeks. How am I going to fit everything in?

38

The next week is taken up with guests and a wedding. It's all hands to the pump. Sylvie, Rose, and Yvette are once again a great help, with Alice in charge of operations. Xavier and Pedro are busy organising the parking, and Gus is in control of keeping the dogs in the kennels around the back of the Chateau. We don't need any more puppies. My only task is to answer any queries and show guests to their tables. The weather is perfect, now that it has started to cool down a little, and the day passes without incident. By 10.30 pm, I've had enough, and my feet are killing me. I step out of my shoes and walk barefoot on the cold kitchen floor. Rose says as she places the last of the glasses into the dishwasher, "You look tired, Laura, why don't you go to bed."

"But," I protest, "the bride and groom, and the guests that are staying over are still sat outside drinking."

Xavier arrives from the cellar with more champagne and having overheard Rose's observation looks at me and says, "Bed. Look at your ankles — zey are very swollen. Go and rest, Laura. Please. I will stay until everyone 'as gone, and I will be back to do breakfast wiz Mama and Gus."

"Thank you," I say gratefully and waddle upstairs for some much-needed sleep. I plop onto my big bed and look over to my nursery corner, still no crib and only eight weeks to go. Sighing, I manoeuvre onto my side and drift off, listening to the sound of laughter floating through the open window.

I'm in the back of Xavier's big truck. I look around as another searing pain travels through my belly. I begin to pant, but the sound of bleating startles me — goats. I'm sharing the back of the truck with four goats! I drag myself to the back door to look out of the window. Snow! It's at least three feet deep, and we're stuck. "Xavier! Help!" My shouting wakes me up. Where am I? Confused, I slowly gather myself together and sit up.

I'm startled once more as my bedroom door flies open. Xavier strides over to me, asking, "Laura, what's wrong?"

I wince as our son begins to dance on my bladder. Pointing over to the bathroom, I say, "Toilet."

Xavier places his arms around me and helps me out of bed, guiding me to the door. When I return, a glass of fresh, ice-cold water is waiting for me. Xavier hands it to me and says, "Drink." I do as I'm told and then climb back onto my bed.

"Why are you here?" I demand, sliding under the duvet. "What time is it?"

"It's only 5 am, and I'm sleeping on ze landing…"

"You can't do that…"

"I 'ave ze camp bed. Ze guests don't want breakfast until 10 am. Go back to sleep."

"Get in," I say, pulling the covers down for him.

He hesitates briefly, then climbs onto my bed, asking, "Why did you shout for me?"

I shake my head as the remnants of my crazy dream flash through my mind. "I'm sorry," I say. "It was only a dream, get some rest." He lays beside me, and I drift off, listening to his soft breathing.

When I wake again, Xavier has gone, and I can smell coffee. I roll over to see a tray by the window, laden with pastries, orange juice and a thermos full of coffee. A glance at my phone informs me it's almost noon. I sit up and stretch, then remember my guests. Noah begins to wake up, and I need to rush to the bathroom once more. On my return I hear voices outside, followed by car engines. I waddle to the window to watch my guests leaving, the newlywed's car is at the front of the procession as they head off on their honeymoon. I tuck into my brunch and enjoy the brief decadence before dressing to begin the process of tidying the Chateau.

When I step out onto the landing I find Alice and Rose filling the trolley with dirty laundry from the guest rooms. Rose looks up, "Good morning, how are you feeling?"

"Much better, thank you. Let me help."

"We've almost finished; there's not much left to do."

"Oh, okay, I'll go and check the marquee…"

"Xavier and Pedro have already cleaned it," Alice says. "Please go and rest." Feeling at a loss, I head down the stairs.

Downstairs, I find that the Chateau has returned to normal. All the trappings from the wedding have gone, except for the floral arrangements, which still look amazing. I wander outside and sit on the front terrace with Shadow and Freckles beside me, and I wonder where Xavier and Gus are. Shadow stands and sniffs the air, then sets off in a hurry towards the tree-lined drive. Freckles follows him, and soon both dogs are digging frantically. I call them, but they continue with their quest. Of course! It dawns on me, truffles. It's the beginning of the truffle season. When I reach them, Shadow has a neat row of four small truffles, while Freckles continues to dig random holes. I pick up Shadow's harvest and call both dogs back then text Xavier.

Truffles. X

He quickly replies.

Yes, I have already been out wiz Pepper, but zey are not quite ready yet. X

I retreat out of the autumnal sun to the shade of the terrace and put the dogs inside. Before I have the chance to get comfortable, my phone rings; the caller ID is showing an unknown number. "Hello?" I answer.

"Miss Mackley, it's Franco. Sorry to bother you on a Sunday afternoon."

"Franco, thank you for ringing. Please, call me Laura. Do you have any more information?"

"Yes, Robert has been following the messy digital trail that the two men have left behind, and we have a name. Philip LeBeau. Does that mean anything to you?"

"Oh my God!" I say, shock stealing my breath for a moment. "Yes! He is Gus's grandfather; he tried to get custody of Gus. Thankfully, he failed. What has he got to do with the two conmen?"

"They are his frontmen," Franco replies.

My brain is still trying to play catch-up. "Sorry, what do you mean?"

"Philip LeBeau is the man behind the attempted break-ins; those two men are on his payroll," Franco confirms.

"But… but what does he want?" I ask, as a dark thought crosses my mind. "Do you think he's still trying to get Gus?"

"I don't know, but I doubt it," Franco says. "I think there must be something in your Chateau that he desperately wants."

"But what, and how would he know what's in my Chateau?" Panic begins to take over, and I take a deep breath to try to calm myself.

"Valentina told me that he tried to buy it from you when you first arrived…"

"Yes. Yes, he did," I say, rubbing my forehead with my hand as I try and think. "I still have the letter somewhere."

"Good, send me a photo of it. I believe LeBeau is a distant relative of the old General. Is that correct?"

"Yes, I think his grandfather was a cousin. What should I do now?"

"Nothing. Leave it with us. We're getting close; we'll soon have this wrapped up." I end the call and sit back, staring at my phone.

Philip LeBeau. I thought we'd seen the last of him. I wonder what he wants. He knows that I've discovered the Bugatti. He was, after all, at the auction when it sold. I'm sure he will know about the other treasures I sold too. Hmm, what else have I found recently? The gold bar. It wasn't worth a vast sum but will help towards the attic conversion. My ponderings are interrupted by Xavier's truck arriving. He jumps out with Gus, and they look at each other, grinning, "What are you two up to?" I ask.

Both of their grins fade slightly, and Xavier motions to Gus, who says, "Erm, nothing. I'm… erm, a bit stuck with my English homework. Will you help me, please?"

"Sure, what do you have to do?" I ask, heaving myself up and waddle after him into the kitchen where he closes the door and pulls a chair out for me. I plonk myself next to him and help him to compile a short story based on a series of pictures; it's pretty simple, and I'm not at all sure why he needed my help. His English is better than my French. A short while later Xavier appears, wearing a stupid grin and offering Gus a thumbs-up sign. My suspicions raised, I ask, "Just a minute, what are you two up to?"

Gus jumps up excitedly and takes my hand. "Come," he says. He leads me upstairs, along the landing to my bedroom door. "You can go in now." I look over to Xavier, who smiles then opens the door. I walk inside and my eyes land on a beautiful swinging crib. It's stunning. Xavier smiles at me, and I'm putty. I walk towards him and wrap my arms around his neck.

"Thank you, it's amazing. Have you made it?"

"No, I've restored it, wiz ze 'elp of Gus and Adam."

"Thank you, both of you. Thank you," I whisper, trying to quell my mounting emotions. I clear my throat, combating tears. "Where did it come from?"

"Here, right here in the Chateau," Gus exclaims. "Aunt Mary gave it to Nana when I was born."

"So, you slept in it when you were tiny?"

"No," Xavier says. "It was in poor condition, and Mama wouldn't let me use it. But now it is mended, and back where it belongs, for ze children of ze Chateau to use. We 'ave used natural materials, and it is safe for ze baby," he adds proudly.

I walk over and slide my fingers over the smooth wooden rails. I can see where new pieces of wood have been seamlessly blended in with the old, which only adds to its beauty.

Gus pulls out a neat wooden peg and gently rocks the crib to and fro. Smiling, he says, "See, it swings. I helped with the varnish."

I smile and hug him.

"Now we 'ave ze crib," says Xavier, "all we need is ze baby."

39

It's noticeably cooler now that we have reached early October. The tourists are dwindling, and the campsite is quiet once more, though I'm expecting a young couple who are due to arrive later today. They are here for the rock-climbing. It's the lull between the end of summer and the beginning of the skiing season. I take a quick look at my favourite website before dashing off to my antenatal appointment. It's now thirty-three weeks, and Noah is the size of butternut squash. He also weighs as much as a laptop, and don't I know it! At the antenatal appointment, the midwife informs me that his head has already engaged. "Does this mean he's going to be born soon?"

"No," she says, "it's not unusual for the head to engage early in your first pregnancy; don't worry about it. It can get a little uncomfortable, though."

"Uncomfortable!" I protest. "It feels as though I've got an elephant sat on my bladder!"

The midwife only smiles and asks, "Are you ready for the arrival of your baby? We recommend that you have a bag packed ready for the hospital with your notes and any phone numbers that you might need after week thirty; just in case."

"I've got the essentials," I say, "but my bag isn't packed. I'm not due for another six or seven weeks." A thought that has been worrying me raises its head, and I ask, "What happens if snow blocks the roads, and I can't get to the hospital?"

"Yes, it happens sometimes," the midwife confirms. "Be prepared and check the weather forecast. Have you got a 4x4 with snow tyres and chains?" She asks.

"Erm, I haven't got chains, but we have a 4x4, and a truck," I say.

She nods then says, "Also, keep a shovel and some essentials in your car. But if in doubt don't travel; it's safer to stay at home than risk getting stuck. Remember, be prepared but don't dwell on it; it's unlikely to happen. Have you been to your antenatal classes?"

I shake my head and say, "I, erm, I just didn't get around to it."

"Well, you should. Here," the midwife says, handing me a card with a name and number printed on it. "This is the lady that coordinates the classes, ring before it's too late."

I leave the surgery feeling like a naughty child and ring the number as soon as I reach home.

The woman informs me that there are no spaces left now. I am, however, allowed to book myself onto a tour of the maternity ward and delivery suite for the following week. The efficient sounding woman also advises me to buy a copy of a DVD that she just so happens to sell, and download it to my laptop. It covers all of the topics from the antenatal class, a type of virtual course. Even better, I can learn everything in the comfort of my own home without the hassle of fighting to park at the hospital.

Once it downloads, I make myself as comfortable as I can and begin to watch. It's pretty routine; it starts with recommending a healthy lifestyle, listing all of the food and activities that pregnant women should avoid. The next episode is informative, charting the week by week development of the baby and the changes that pregnant women will undergo. Currently, I may experience heartburn, backache, insomnia and much more. The list is extensive, and I'm sure I have most of them. Allegedly, Noah may now have hair on his head, and his testicles should have descended into his scrotum. Xavier will like that snippet of information! Oh, he will be born with blue eyes, and it could take a few months for them to turn brown like his father's. As I'm about to settle down to chapter three, Preparing for the Birth, the alarm on the gatepost informs me that my guests have arrived; the birth will have to wait.

I pull on a jumper and waddle over to the campsite with Shadow and Freckles in tow to introduce myself. Once I've shown my guests the facilities, I waddle back to find Xavier in the kitchen. "I was going to greet ze guests, but you beat me to it."

"Yes, apparently exercise is good for me, even though I'm out of breath."

"Did you see ze midwife today?"

"Yes, I should be attending antenatal classes by now. I've rung the hospital, but they are full. So, I've downloaded their DVD. Did you know that Noah's testicles are now in his scrotum?"

He stops what he's doing and stares at me, open-mouthed, "I should 'ope so! Where else would zey be? In 'is ears?"

Okay, perhaps I asked for that. I grin, saying, "I've watched the first two episodes. I was just about to move onto preparing for the birth, would you care to join me?" After his usual shrug, we settle down on the sofa and start to watch. It begins with the expected — birth plans, breathing exercises and bag packing, but swiftly takes a personal turn as a detailed, labelled diagram of lady parts fills the screen, and the narrator suggests massaging your perineum daily from thirty-four weeks onwards. Well, that's next week's job then!

At this gem of information, Xavier jumps up and says, "Erm, I've just remembered. I 'ave to go and check ze vines before it gets dark." He then turns and leaves me alone, staring at the vagina, filling my laptop screen.

I sigh and turn it off. If Xavier can't even look at an image on a screen, how is he going to help me when it comes to the real thing, giving birth? I wonder if he was present when Gus was born? I very much doubt it. I think back to early spring and the lambing season. He didn't bat an eyelid when he was delivering lambs; this can't be much different. Who am I kidding? I remember how tense it was when Jenny and I helped Jackie to deliver baby Frances. I've assisted delivering several babies, and a few lambs, and I've done a short course in obstetrics. Why am I even watching this? It's common sense, and I know all of this stuff. So, why do I feel so inadequate? They always say that nurses make the worst patients. I will still go and take a look around the maternity ward next week. It will be useful to know where I'm going and familiarise myself with the surroundings, though I won't be staying very long; twenty-four hours, assuming all goes to plan.

40

Xavier calls in the next morning to collect Shadow as the truffle season starts in earnest. As he leaves, I ask, "Are you taking Freckles?"

"No, 'e is a liability. Shadow and Pepper will do better wizout ze distraction. Besides, 'is job is to look after you."

"I'm okay, and I won't be alone today. Adam is coming to do some more work in the attic. Look, here he is now," I say as Adam's truck pulls up outside. Xavier goes out to greet him, and the two men exchange a few words before Xavier disappears with his troop of dogs.

Adam enters with coils of brightly coloured wire, which he takes up to the attic, and it's not long before I hear banging coming from above me. It's a good job that I don't have any guests staying today. It's been a while since I've seen Alice. I think I'll take a walk over to the farmhouse, no doubt she will be turning out cakes and pastries with Rose for the catering business. I arrive to find the kitchen door closed, which is unusual. I know the weather's much cooler now, but it will be hot in her kitchen. I let myself in and call, "Hello!" The kitchen is empty, and the oven is cold. I wonder if she's at Rose's house. I decide to send her a text.

Hi, I called in to see you, are you with Rose? x

I close the door behind me and walk back to the Chateau via the vines. The damage to the first row doesn't look as bad as it did, and the rest of the grapes look plump and juicy; it's almost harvest time again. I think back to last year, my first harvest, it was a sight to behold. Lots of the locals turned out to help, Jenny and Enzo were here too. And what a party we had afterwards! Jenny can't make it this time. She's saving her holiday for when Noah is due. And Enzo! Huh! Who knows what he's doing? And, quite frankly, I don't care. My phone pings with a text reply from Alice.

I was with Rose earlier, and now I'm with a friend. Is everything okay? X

I think the friend will be Monsieur le Maire. I'm so pleased for her.

Yes, everything's fine, have a lovely afternoon x

I stop by the pond and rest while Freckles splashes about in the shallows. However, it's not long before Noah decides to stomp on my bladder, which sends me waddling home to the toilet.

"Laura! Laura! I'm so glad you're back. Come and see what I've unearthed," Adam shouts as I reach the door.

"Can it wait? I'm desperate for the loo," I mutter as I rush past him. Five minutes later, I'm standing next to him in the attic, peering down a hole in the floorboards. "Oh! Is it another radio set?"

"Possibly," he replies, bending down and lifting the old wooden box out of its dusty hiding place. He wipes his hand across its surface, removing a thick layer of dust before slowly opening the lid. Neither of us speaks as we look at the weird contraption.

"Is it a typewriter?" I ask, then read the word printed on the inside of its lid. Enigma. "What does 'Enigma' mean?" I look over at Adam, who stares back at me, speechless.

Adam opens his mouth but forms no coherent words, only a muffled croak. He then clears his throat and tries again, "No way! It can't be, can it?"

"What? What can't it be?"

"Well, if I'm not mistaken, I think it's an Enigma machine," he says, standing back and looking at me with a shocked expression.

"Isn't that what the Germans used in the war to encrypt messages?"

"Yes, it is."

"What is it doing here, in my attic?" I stare at it in disbelief.

"Erm, good question."

I point to the hole, "Is there anything else down there?"

Adam gets on his hands and knees and shines his lamp into the gloom under the floorboards. "Can't see anything," he reports. "But I'll be lifting some more of these boards later for the rewiring, so I'll have a good look. What are you going to do with it?"

"I don't know. Will you carry it down to the kitchen for me so I can have a good look at it? I need to consult Google."

A short while later and I have the information from the web. It is indeed an Enigma cypher machine; Adam was correct. It was used by the German military to turn communications into a code, which was almost impossible to decipher. Although, Alan Turin and his colleagues, with help from some Polish mathematicians, built a machine called the Bombe which managed to achieve the impossible and helped us to win the war. Wow! I wonder how, and why it found its way here? I continue searching for information and try to compare it to some of the images on my screen. It takes a while as there seem to be several variations and manufacturers.

At last, I find a similar one, and it's for sale. I screw my eyes tight and open them again as I'm sure I'm not seeing straight. Two hundred and twenty-one thousand dollars! No way! That can't be correct. I compare the two machines again, and I'm confident it's the same. I close the lid on my laptop and stare at the device sitting on the table. What am I supposed to do now? Before I have a chance to think, Adam enters the kitchen, carrying a small leather case.

"Erm, Laura. I've found this," he looks at me worriedly and places the item on the table next to the Enigma machine.

"What is it?"

"Open it."

I do as he suggests, lifting the lid to reveal a panel with nobs and switches and a headset. "It's another radio receiver."

"Yes, it is, but it's also German; look at the writing." He pulls out a chair and flops down by my side. "You know what this means, don't you?"

"Right now, Adam, I don't know anything! My brain is fried."

He puts his hand on my shoulder, "Yes, it's a lot to take in, but I think these belonged to a collaborator." He sits back and puts his hands in his lap and stares at the two objects on the table.

"A… what?"

"Here in the Chateau, during the war, someone was on the other side."

Puzzled, I ask, "Germans? Here in the Chateau—"

He looks at me and sighs, "No, they probably weren't Germans. I've heard rumours that some members of the resistance were collaborators; they spied for the Germans."

"A spy! Here, in my Chateau?" I close my eyes, sit back in my chair and begin to practise my breathing techniques; I need to think of Noah and not let myself get stressed.

Adam stands up and once again puts a reassuring hand on my shoulder. "Laura, are you okay?" He asks. I don't speak, only nod as I continue counting my breaths. Adam picks up my phone and hands it to me, saying, "Ring Xavier, please."

Feeling better, I look at him and smile. "No need, I'm fine." His worried features soften, and I continue, "So, a spy; but who?"

Adam shrugs, and I have to smile as an image of Xavier comes into my head, followed quickly by a little boy with brown curly hair and chocolate brown eyes, standing beside his father. Both shrugging as they tell me a tale. This baby is going to have his parents wrapped around his little finger. I shake my head and try to think. A spy. Who could that have been, and how do I find out? Adam breaks into my thoughts when he says, "I'll go back up and carry on. Will you be okay?"

"Yes, thank you. As long as you don't find anything else."

41

Thankfully, Adam doesn't find anything else lurking in the attic and leaves before tea to spend some time with his children. I'm sitting in the kitchen, pondering my discoveries when the back door opens. Xavier walks in with a grin on his face, followed by three muddy dogs, and drops his bag on the kitchen surface. "Success…" he says, before spotting the machines on the table. "Oh, what are zose?"

"Hello Xavier, have you had a good day?"

"Erm, yes… Laura, where did you get zose?"

I look at him, then back at the floor, which is now covered in muddy boot prints and let out a long sigh. "Adam," I say. "He found them under the floorboards in the attic."

He walks across and touches the Enigma machine. He asks, "What is it?"

"It's an Enigma machine from the war—"

He doesn't let me finish and interrupts, "Ze Germans used zem to encrypt communications; what is it doing 'ere?"

"Good question; along with a German radio set." I gesture to it. "Adam thinks there may have been a spy in the Chateau."

"No…"

"What other explanation is there?"

"Erm, I don't know," his brow creases and he continues, "perhaps zey captured it, or somezing."

"Mm, if only these walls could talk. I wonder if Aunt Mary knew about it?"

"No, she didn't arrive until after ze liberation. She couldn't 'ave known. Anyway, you can't ask 'er now," Xavier points out.

"I suppose we'll never know; another mystery." I stand to go and get a mop to clean up the mess on the floor when an idea pops into my head. "The diary, Father Flory's diary. I wonder if we can find any information from that?" The mess can wait, I retrieve the diary from the library and hand it to Xavier, saying, "Here, you look. You'll be able to read it quicker than me." I put the kettle on and make us both a hot chocolate and feed the dogs while Xavier sits leafing through the book. Ten minutes later, I ask, "Have you found anything yet?" He continues reading and shakes his head. I sit for a while then waddle over to the bag of truffles and empty them onto the draining board. I sort them into three piles according to size, and it's an excellent start to the new season. Curious, I ask, "Where have you got to?"

"Ze plane crash…" He carries on reading for a short while then lifts his eyes and stares at me, before sliding the open diary across the table, saying, "Read zis." I pick it up and begin to read.

September 1943

I was over at the Chateau earlier today. General De Ford's cousin, Gerart, is still here. He was only supposed to be staying for a couple of weeks, but it's been over two months now since he arrived. I do wonder about him. It may only be in my imagination, but too many things have gone wrong since his arrival. The two airmen, Harry and Norman, were captured, and their driver killed. Someone must have leaked the information to the Germans.

I put the book down and look at Xavier, who is looking back at me with a morose expression. "I don't remember reading this before," I say.

"Well, zere is so much of it, you can't remember everyzing."

"So, do you think this Gerart was the spy?"

"It's possible." He stands and walks behind me and puts his arms around my middle. "Don't dwell on zis. 'Ow is our son?" I melt and lean back into him.

"Heavy."

"I will make supper and zen give you ze massage, yes?"

I wake up the following morning wrapped in Xavier's arms, with my phone ringing. By the time I've struggled free, it's stopped, and I have a missed call which only says withheld number. Well, it can't be that important. It's probably someone trying to sell me something or wants me to change my energy provider. I make scrambled eggs with truffles for breakfast, delicious and very decadent. "What are you doing today?" Xavier asks as he walks into the kitchen.

"Oh, I'm going on a guided tour of the maternity unit at the hospital, would you like to come?"

"Sorry," a look of regret crosses his face, "I 'ave a man coming to mend ze tractor, and work to do in ze vineyard."

On my way to the hospital, my phone rings again, and it's another withheld number. "Hello?" I say.

"Hello, Miss Mackley, er, Laura, it's Marco."

"Marco, hello, did you ring earlier?"

"Yes," he says apologetically. "Sorry to bother you, can you talk?"

"Yes, I'm alone. Have you got any more information?"

"Yes. I've spoken at length with Philip Le Beau, and I'm getting somewhere at last. He says you have some things that belonged to his grandfather in the attic, and he wants them back."

"What things, exactly?"

"He wouldn't say." I could hear the shrug in his voice. "He only said that it was a personal loose end that he needed to attend to."

"The attic is empty now; there's nothing left up there."

"Yes, I've already told him that, but he's insistent that there is still something up there." I hesitate for a few moments as I wonder what can still be up there, is something else hidden? Or could it be the Enigma machine and radio? "Laura, are you still there?"

"Yes, sorry, I was only thinking. What does Le Beau want to do?"

"He wants access to the attic. Then he says he will leave you alone."

"Just a thought, but could you tell me what his grandfather's name was?"

"No, he didn't say, why?"

"Just a hunch, will you ask him if he was called Gerart by any chance?"

"Why?" I spend the next five minutes filling Marco in about the Enigma machine and German radio and the possibility that Gerart might be his grandfather. Afterwards, Marco says, "Laura, I'll find out and ring you back."

I walk around the maternity unit in a trance, taking very little notice of the information the midwife is telling me. My head once again is elsewhere. Poor Harry and Norman, did Le Beau's grandfather, Gerart, have something to do with their capture? And the death of their driver? What else did he do to sabotage operations? I'm startled out of my thoughts when I hear, "Any questions?" What, did somebody say something? I blink at the midwife in confusion. "Erm, Mademoiselle Mackley, do you have any questions?" The midwife asks, having to repeat herself.

"Erm, no. No, thank you," I stutter as quickly as possible, trying to hide the fact that I haven't taken anything in and turn to leave. I climb back into my Yeti and drive out of the car park. "Well, Noah," I say to my belly, "that was a waste of time." I look at the clock and time my journey home, at least I'll know how long the trip takes.

As I turn into the drive, Marco rings back. "Laura," he says. "Le Beau won't tell me his grandfather's name, so I've checked some records online, and his grandfather was indeed Gerart Henri Le Beau. So, the story fits."

"Do you think he was a spy?"

"I can't say, but Philip Le Beau wants the items that you've found."

"Did you tell him about them?"

"No, I gave nothing away, though he is under the impression that they remain hidden."

"Why do you think he wants them?"

Marco pauses in thought before saying, "Well, they will be of considerable value."

"Yes, I've checked; they are. What should we do?"

"Nothing," is his instant reply, "let him sweat for a while; let's see what he does."

"But Marco, what if he sends those men back? I'm having a baby in six weeks; I don't need any more stress right now."

"He won't, and he knows we're on to him. Trust me; this will work in your favour."

42

I don't hear back from Marco for over a week, and life continues at its usual fast pace. The grape harvest is well underway, and I'm not allowed to help, apart from driving the truck over to deliver refreshments to the gang. As usual, lots of locals have turned out to help, and there is a party atmosphere. We're holding the mandatory vendange celebration on Saturday night at the Chateau. Alice is in charge with the assistance of Rose and Yvette.

It's a shame Jenny can't be here with Jacques, but she'll be arriving in three weeks and staying for a while. I'm looking forward to seeing her again but can't say the same about giving birth. I'll be glad when it's all over, and I have my little Noah here in my arms. I'm thirty-five weeks now, where has the time gone? He is the size of a pineapple and about as long as he will get; from here on, he only has to put on another pound of baby fat. My uterus has grown to about a thousand times its original size, and don't I know it! I have to visit the local midwife every two weeks now. She's happy that everything is okay, but I'm beginning to get a little impatient. My breasts are getting huge and have started leaking colostrum. I feel like an elephant. I haven't told anyone, but I'm spending ten minutes in the hot tub without the bubbles on before I go to bed; the feeling of weightlessness is such a relief. I've turned the temperature down so that Noah doesn't overheat.

I'm also beginning to feel superfluous to requirements just now as I'm officially on maternity leave. Alice is already preparing for the Christmas events; the old folks' party and several local office celebrations are in the diary, though I'm finding it challenging to take a back seat. It's taken me eighteen months of love, sweat, and tears to get to this point. I'm still captain of this ship where decisions are concerned, but I've had to learn to step back with the physical work.

I'm planning to return to full duties when Noah is six weeks old. I've put a notice up in the village that I'm looking for a part-time nanny. I've had two applicants so far; one is a village girl, Lucie, and the other is a young mother, Millie, who has a toddler. I've interviewed both and can't make my mind up. Millie will have to bring her son with her sometimes, which might be useful for Noah. He'll have to learn to share from an early age, and she already has experience with babies. Lucie, on the other hand, has no experience but is flexible; I'll have to decide soon. A sharp knock on the door takes me by surprise. Everyone is over in the vineyard, harvesting the grapes. Perhaps they require more refreshments? I waddle into the hall and open the door. I stand rooted to the spot, staring at the man on my doorstep. He has a sickly smile pasted on his face. Phillip Le Beau.

"Miss Mackley, please forgive the intrusion, but I was hoping that we could come to some arrangement."

"Oh, Monsieur Le Beau, I… err, wasn't expecting guests. What sort of… err, arrangement have you got in mind?" Think, Laura, think! "Would you like to make an appointment with my estate manager?"

"No, Miss Mackley, this doesn't concern him; it's you I'd like to see."

"Then, perhaps you should meet me at my solicitor's office, Monsieur Bertrand, in the village; you may remember him?"

"That won't be necessary," he says. "It's a simple matter that you and I can rectify between ourselves."

I hesitate, look over my shoulder and see the three dogs standing to attention a few feet behind me, and I know I'm not in any danger from this man. Beau would have him on the floor in no time, then Shadow and Freckles would quickly join in with the melee. *Breathe Laura*, I tell myself. *You can do this.* I've taken this man on before and won. I can do it again. "Monsieur Le Beau, do come in; if you can get past the dogs."

"Please, call me Phillip, and you have no cause for concern, I wish you no harm." He steps into the hall and looks first at the dogs and then back to me and with a nervous cough, follows me into the drawing-room. Beau is instantly at my side, his eyes never leaving Le Beau, while Shadow closely follows my visitor, keeping in step with him. Once seated, Shadow sits directly in front of Le Beau and stares at him. "Miss Mackley, thank you for, err, seeing me."

"You didn't give me much choice, did you?"

He ignores my curt reply and continues, "Congratulations, I didn't know you were expecting."

"What do you want Le Beau?"

"Well, you see, it's a delicate matter. My grandfather stayed here for a while during the war. He worked for the resistance you know, and was awarded a medal for his bravery." He begins to relax a little and sits back into his chair, expecting me to comment. However, I don't, so he sits forwards again and continues, "But, he left in rather a hurry and didn't manage to take all of his possessions with him."

He looks at the floor, almost squirming, and I can't stop myself from saying, "Well, why was that, I wonder?"

He looks up, and his eyes make contact with mine, but he quickly looks away again. Le Beau's eyes land on the piano, and he then changes the subject, "So, this is the famous piano that plays by itself."

Impatient, I say, "Get to the point or leave."

This comment gets his attention, and he sits up straight, "Laura, may I call you Laura?" I don't respond, so he continues, "I believe that there are a couple of items in the attic that belonged to my late grandfather, and I would like them back. Please."

At last, he's got to the point, but I have no intention of making this easy for him; I'm enjoying myself too much. "The attic is empty now; all of the items that were up there have either been sold or thrown away. Sorry, but you've had a wasted journey."

He frowns, beginning to appear perplexed but recovers quickly and continues, "I believe that these were hidden items, and it was my grandfather's dying wish that they returned to me. You do understand that I must honour the wishes of a dead man, don't you?"

"What are these precious items? And where were they hidden?" These questions have the desired effect of causing him to squirm even more, and I try to stop myself from appearing smug.

"I'm not exactly sure," he says cagily, "but I believe it was electrical equipment of some type."

"Well, I'm certain that it won't be of any use now, even if we manage to find its hiding place." I'm having way too much fun at his expense but can't help myself. "Where do you suggest we look?"

"Oh, Miss Mackley, I don't expect you to help me to search for it in your condition." He looks at me as earnestly as he can, saying, "If you allow me access to the attic, I will look for it myself."

I shake my head, trying to look regretful, "I couldn't possibly allow a guest to wander into the attic alone; it would contravene my health and safety regulations."

"My daughter stayed here for a while, but you know that don't you?" He asks.

"Yes, did she manage to get into the attic for you?" I raise my eyebrows in mock surprise.

"Is that why she was here in the first place, to retrieve your electrical equipment?"

Phillip Le Beau shakes his head. "Miss Mackley; if you will only allow me access. I will be out of your life, and promise never to bother you again," he says, beginning to lose his charm.

I'm beginning to get bored now and decide it's now or never. "Monsieur Le Beau," I say as calmly as I can, "I believe that the two items that you are looking for are now elsewhere. That is if you are referring to the German Enigma machine and radio set that your grandfather, Gerart Henri Le Beau used to betray his fellow countrymen."

Vindication washes over me as I watch the man visibly change — his features harden, and he stands and strides over to the window then back to stand in front of me in a threatening manner. Beau reacts immediately and approaches him, baring his teeth; Freckles copies him, while Shadow rushes to my side.

"Call your dog's off. Now!" Le Beau says, looking uneasy.

A single, loud, low note resonates out from the piano, startling him, and he stares at it with an alarmed look on his face. I smile at him, coldly, then say, "So, Monsieur Le Beau, you were right about something; this is the piano that plays by itself." His mouth opens and closes without making a sound. "Are you ready to share the truth with me now, or do I need to deploy my dogs to see you out?"

He sits back down and visibly deflates, hesitating while gathering his thoughts. "Erm, my grandfather," he says, "told me that he obtained the Enigma machine and radio set from a German that he captured. Have you still got them?"

I stand up and make my way to the library and return with the diary, which I put on the small table between us. "Father Flory wrote this diary," I say. "He was the local priest during the war." I pick it back up and turn to the page that implicates his grandfather's involvement. I hand it to him.

He looks at me and hesitates before taking it from me, then fishes a pair of glasses out of his top pocket and begins to read. He then removes his glasses and sits back, looking smug and says, "This isn't firm evidence."

"And this isn't a court of law. You chose that route last time and lost. I suggest that you learn from it and move on. What do you genuinely want Le Beau?"

He sighs and stands then walks over to the window, looking out over the estate. "I want this to remain a secret." He runs his hand over his face, "My grandfather's stupid actions can't deface the great Le Beau name. We could sell the items and share the profit, then go our separate ways."

I relax, knowing that I now have the upper hand. "Le Beau," I say. "You may remember when I first came here that Aunt Mary left the Chateau and all of its contents in her will to me. The very same Chateau, estate, and all of its contents that you offered me the measly sum of 500,000 Euros for."

Le Beau turns away from the window to face me. "Yes, I know it was left to you in your aunts will; an aunt that you weren't even aware existed. I contested the will. It is my birth right! I am a genuine descendant of General De Ford; you are merely an incomer. The Bugatti should have stayed in the family; it should be mine!" Le Beau's voice escalates in anger, and he balls his fists at his side.

Once more, Beau bares his teeth and snarls at Le Beau. However, his threatening behaviour doesn't alarm me; a single command from me, and Beau will deal with him. Calmly, I say, "Le Beau, I do sympathise, but Gus will get his share of the estate – in time; but right now, I am the custodian of this Chateau and will always endeavour to do what is in its best interests."

"Humph! You mean what's in your best interests…"

"Enough!" A voice in the hall booms through the door, "I've heard enough Le Beau! Get out before I call the police!"

Le Beau looks over to see Monsieur Le Maire and Alice, who is now standing in the doorway. His demeanour instantly changes to one of sickly-sweetness as he spies the gentleman, "Ah, Monsieur Le Maire, how lovely to see you again. I was discussing a business matter with Miss Mackley."

Alice rushes to my side and puts her motherly arms around my shoulder while Monsieur Le Maire gives Le Beau a cold stare. "I heard enough of the conversation to know what you were discussing." A disgusted expression crosses his face as he asks, "What did you expect to achieve? The Chateau belongs to Mademoiselle Mackley, so I suggest you leave if you know what's good for you."

An awkward silence follows that I decide to use to my advantage. "Thank you Monsieur Le Maire; Le Beau is here to retrieve a German Enigma machine and radio set that his grandfather, Gerart Henri Le Beau, used in the resistance; he was a spy."

Le Beau sputters, "No. No, you are mistaken—"

Monsieur Le Maire cuts him off, mid-sentence. "Silence!" He barks, then looks at me and continues in a softer voice, "Laura, is this true?" I nod and recount the story of my latest find and show him the diary entry that Father Flory wrote. Alice looks on in disbelief. Xavier hadn't allegedly informed her. Le Beau, now at a loss for words, looks on with increasing unease when Monsieur Le Maire asks, "Laura, what do you intend to do with the Enigma machine and radio set?"

All eyes land on me but I'm not concerned; I have already made my decision. "I have contacted a museum in Paris, and they are delighted by the find and have arranged for someone to come out to collect the items."

"So, you're going to sell them; just as I thought!" Le Beau sneers.

"No," I correct him. "I've donated them. They are not mine to sell; they belong to the French people. We need to remember the stories of the brave souls that risked everything; like the story of your grandfather." I look Le Beau in the eyes, but he averts his gaze to the floor.

"Yes, about that particular story; Laura, have you told it to anyone else?" Monsieur Le Maire asks, looking at me hopefully.

Le Beau looks up from the carpet and stares at me.

"No," I say. "No, I haven't. The only other person that knows is Xavier. Oh, and the private detective that I used."

Le Beau looks over to Monsieur Le Maire expectantly.

"Well, that is good news, my dear," Monsieur Le Maire says, looking at me. He then turns his whole body towards Le Beau and with a warning tone continues, "I'm sure that Miss Mackley would be prepared to keep your disreputable, little secret in return for certain conditions." Le Beau nods, though doesn't say anything and his shoulders sag as he continues to listen. "Good. You will never contact Miss Mackley again, or any of her family; this includes Mrs Besnard, Xavier, and Gus Besnard. You will not try to make contact via a third party, and you will never set foot in this Chateau or the estate ever again. Have I made myself clear?"

Le Beau again nods then opens his mouth to speak. He hesitates then looks over to me and asks, "And what about the pesky detective, will you call him off?"

"Consider it done," Monsieur Le Maire answers on my behalf. "Now leave and mark my words; if I ever have cause to speak with you again on this matter, it won't end well."

Le Beau looks at me and bows formally before turning and making a hasty retreat. I sag into the chair behind me and begin to tremble. "Laura, are you okay? Alice, my dear, should we call for the doctor?" Monsieur Le Maire asks.

Alice rushes to my side, offering her comfort. "No," she says, "put the kettle on and make Laura a cup of sweet tea, she will be fine; she's a strong young woman."

"Indeed, she is. I've just witnessed that for myself," Monsieur Le Maire replies over his shoulder on the way to the kitchen.

43

Alice assists me upstairs for a rest after I've drunk my tea, and I try to get comfortable. Unfortunately, the nagging ache in my lower back makes the task difficult. I begin to relive the experience in my head and wonder if it was the correct thing to do.

"You should be asleep," Xavier whispers as he enters my bedroom. He pulls up a chair and sits beside me, taking hold of my hand. "'Ow dare 'e turn up like zat and scare you…"

I raise my hand and pick a small bunch of leaves that have got tangled up in his unruly curls and smile, "Don't, he's gone now, and the situation dealt with; in the typical French style."

Xavier smiles and nods, then his features harden, "If 'e ever comes near you again, 'e will live to regret it…"

"Shh, he won't, it's over. How is the vendange?" I ask, trying to change the subject.

"Good, it's good, we will finish zis evening."

"Excellent, go back and get on with it then," I say just as a nasty twinge travels through my lower back, and I wince involuntarily.

"Laura, are you okay?"

"Yes, yes, just backache; I'm struggling to get comfortable. I'll be fine, get back to work."

Reluctantly, he stands. "Mama is staying 'ere wiz you, ring if you need me." He places a gentle kiss on my cheek and turns, waving as he reaches the door. "Please, stay in bed and rest."

Once Xavier's gone, I roll onto my side and place a pillow for my leg to rest on, it seems to help a little, and at last, I fall asleep.

Unexpectedly, I'm in the hospital carpark, and excruciating pains are tearing me apart. I get an uncontrollable urge to push, "Help! Help!" I shout. A man approaches the car and knocks on my window. I press the button to lower the window and begin to yell again, "Help, get the midwife!" I look into the man's face only to find the evil eyes of Le Beau staring back at me.

I awake with a jolt and sit bolt upright in bed. An uncomfortable sensation begins in my lower back and travels around and across my abdomen, tightening, causing even more discomfort. I hold on to my belly and roll forwards, making a groaning sound.

I then feel Alice's arms comfort me as she says, "Laura, are you okay? Breathe. Try to take some deep breaths." I do as she suggests, leaning back into the pillows and begin to take slow, steady breaths. "Good girl, is that better?"

I nod and try to smile as the unpleasant sensation subsides. "I'm sorry, it was only a bad dream; it's gone now."

"Are you sure, should I call the midwife?"

"I'm sure. It's been a difficult day; I'll be fine after I've had a rest." Alice continues to fuss about me, rearranging the covers and plumping the pillows. "Alice, I'm feeling a little nauseous, could I have a cold drink and a sandwich, please?" That should give her something else to do instead of fussing. I lay back down and try to clear my mind of Le Beau and the events of this afternoon. It's over, and I need to put it to rest. I eat my sandwich and place a drop of lavender oil onto the inside of my wrists and take a few deep breaths and remember no more.

It's pitch black when I awake to find Xavier lying asleep on top of the bedclothes. He's still wearing the clothes he had on earlier with yet more leaves stuck in his hair. I climb out of bed and tiptoe to the bathroom, where, to my horror, I find a slimy pink mark in my pants. Oh my God! Am I in labour? Is Noah about to be born? I have a wee and waddle back to my bed, then climb back on beside Xavier. He must be exhausted. I wonder what time they finished last night. I gently pluck the leaves from his tousled locks and stretch to place them on the bedside table. The uncomfortable sensation returns and travels from the bottom of my back, around into my hardening belly.

Is this it? Labour. How will I know? I reach for my tablet and begin my search. Early signs of labour, here we are – The signs of pre-labour: Nausea, yes, I have that. A bloody show, yes, I've had that too. Persistent lower back pain, that's also an affirmative, cramps or tightening of the uterus, yes. Yes, I'm in pre-labour, whatever that is. I read through the list, and it says to contact your midwife if you're less than thirty-seven weeks pregnant; I'm thirty-six weeks now, does that matter? Just one week. I continue reading and decide that I'll try to go back to sleep and see how I am in the morning. I look down onto Xavier's sleeping form, yes, it's the right thing to do; it's only 4.20 am, he must be exhausted.

I close my eyes and try to still my racing mind. Deep, slow breathing helps for a short while, but soon my thoughts return; is my son on his way? Noah. My lovely boy. Another uncomfortable tightening occurs, and I check the time. It's 5.15 am; almost an hour since the last one. I make a note on my phone and try again to relax, but it's impossible; this time I remember I haven't yet packed my bag. It was on my to-do list the day that the fire broke out, but I had graver things to attend to on that particular day. Should I do it now? No, that would require me putting the light on, and I don't want to disturb Xavier. It may be the last decent night's sleep he gets for a while! No, I'll wait until morning.

I run through all of the items that I'm going to need and make a list on my phone. I'm sure I've already made several notes previously but can't find them just now. I satisfy myself by doing more internet research. At thirty-six weeks, Noah is the size of a cabbage, and his lungs are considered mature enough to breathe unaided. Well, that's reassuring. I then go on to read that he would still be premature until thirty-seven weeks. Can I hang on for another week?

My next search is complications of babies born at thirty-six weeks; respiratory distress, sepsis, jaundice, low birth weight, difficulty regulating temperature, the list goes on. My heart rate jumps, and Noah boots me again in the ribs.

Laura, this is not helping! I chastise myself and turn my phone off. Sleep is what I need, what we all need. I inhale from the bottle of lavender by my bedside and lay back down. This time, instead of trying to count my breaths, I listen to Xavier and match my breathing to his steady rhythm. The next time I awake, I find myself alone, but I can hear the shower running in my bathroom. I smile as an image of his naked body glistening with water pops into my head. No, definitely not helping my cause! I sigh and sneak out of bed to make a cup of tea. When I return with the tray, he walks out of the bathroom with a towel wrapped around his waist. "You should be in bed," he chastises. "I was about to make breakfast." As I reach to put the tray on the table, another contraction strikes and I drop it with a loud clatter. "Laura, what's wrong?" He closes the distance between us and takes me in his arms, "Are you in pain? Is it ze baby? Shall I call ze doctor?"

The discomfort gradually subsides, and I sit on the bed, looking at the tea regretfully. Most of it is now sloshing about on the tray. "Sorry, I've spilt the tea."

"Ze tea doesn't matter, what's wrong?"

"I'm not sure. I've been having what I think could be contractions…"

"'Ow long as zis been 'appening?"

"The first one was not long after Le Beau left, then I had what I think was a show in the night, and I think three more contractions since."

"Zat's it, I'm ringing ze doctor," he says and picks his phone up from the table. He gets through and speaks rapidly in French then turns and says, "'E wants to talk wiz you."

I take the phone from him and run through the events of the last twenty-four hours to the local doctor. He asks, "Is the baby still moving?" I tell him that Noah is most definitely still booting me in the ribs, which seems to reassure him. "I would like you to rest for the remainder of your pregnancy. I will ask the midwife to call in to see you today, but, if anything changes ring the hospital."

I end the call, and Xavier takes his phone from me. "Well, what did 'e say, do you 'ave to go to ze 'ospital?"

I lean back into my pillows and sigh, "No, it's nothing to be alarmed about, as long as the baby is still moving. But as a precaution, he is sending the midwife out to see me."

"Is zat all?"

"Yes, and he wants me to rest."

"Good, yes, rest. I want you to rest, stay where you are, and I will bring breakfast." Xavier pulls on a t-shirt and a pair of boxer shorts and walks to the door then turns around and admonishes, "Keep your phone wiz you at all times."

Not long after breakfast, Xavier shows the midwife up to my room. As she walks in she asks, "Laura, how are you, what's been happening?" Once again, I recount my story as she listens. She checks my pulse and blood pressure then produces a Pinard horn, a type of trumpet that she presses into my abdomen to listen to the baby. She looks at her watch, counting Noah's heartbeat.

"Can you 'ear 'im?" Xavier asks anxiously, hovering by the door.

The midwife stands and smiles at him. "Yes, baby sounds to be perfectly fine."

"Is she in labour?"

The midwife once again smiles and says, "It could be the very early stage of labour, we call it latent labour—"

"What is zat?" Xavier interrupts.

I mouth sorry in her direction, and she continues, "It's understandable that you're concerned, but this stage of labour can last days or even a week. It's the time that a woman's cervix is starting to thin in preparation for true labour." She looks back at me. "With you only being thirty-six weeks, we would like to delay the onset of true labour for as long as possible. I could send you to the hospital, where they would probably put you on bed rest. Or, you could stay here in the comfort of your own home, and I would be happy to call in every day. But you must promise to rest."

"'Ospital," Xavier says immediately, but I stare at him in horror.

"No, thank you," I say. "I'd much rather stay here and rest, with your assistance, of course."

The midwife, noticing our exchange asks, "Can someone stay with you?"

"Yes, I will stay," Xavier says.

"But you have work to do," I protest. "Have you finished pressing the grapes?" He doesn't answer, and I know that he can't possibly have finished the mammoth task.

The midwife looks back at me. "Hmm, I don't think you should be alone now. Is there someone else that could come and stay?" I run through my list of friends; Jenny is the obvious choice, but I can't exactly expect her to drop everything and be here in five minutes — she's busy working overtime so that she can come to help when Noah arrives. Alice, Rose, and Yvette are beavering away with the catering side of the business. And Sylvie is busy teaching. "Shall I make arrangements for you to stay in the hospital?" The midwife asks after I fail to come up with an alternative.

Xavier nods in agreement, but I'm not about to give up just yet. "No," I say. "I could ask Lucie, the young girl who has applied for the post of the nanny."

"Can she drive?"

"Yes, she's recently passed her driving test…"

Xavier looks at me, horrified. "You must not let her drive you to ze 'ospital. I will not leave ze estate; ring and I will be wiz you in less zan five minutes."

"Okay, that sounds like a plan. I'll stay while you ring Lucie to make certain," the midwife says.

Five minutes later, everything is to the midwife's liking. Lucie is packing a bag and will be arriving within the hour.

44

Xavier refuses to leave until Lucie arrives, so I put him to good use making up the rear guest room. It feels a little weird, inviting a stranger to come and stay. I've only met Lucie once previously for about half an hour. She seemed like a nice girl, but she's only twenty years old. She left college two years ago, where she did a catering course and has worked in hospitality ever since, though now wants a change. The alarm on the gate post informs me of her arrival. If I'm feeling apprehensive, imagine how she must feel. Xavier opens the front door, and I can hear him talking, I do hope he's behaving. I remember how daunting it was when I arrived here. I wonder if she knew Aunt Mary.

Soon, I hear them climb the stairs, and Xavier shows her into my room. I smile and hold my hand out in her direction, "Lucie, thank you so much for coming at such short notice; I hope it wasn't too inconvenient."

She steps forward, a little awkwardly and smiles back, "I'm glad I was able to help."

"Good, I'll leave you two now. Remember; ring and I will be 'ere in five minutes," Xavier says, dropping a kiss on the top of my head.

"What would you like me to do?" Lucie asks once he's left. "Can I get you anything?"

"Have you had lunch?" I ask, trying to sound upbeat, and attempting to make her feel at ease. She shakes her head, so I continue, "Good, neither have I. Would you make a sandwich and a drink for both of us? Bring it up here, and we can get to know each other a little better."

"I, erm, don't know where you keep things."

"Yes, it's going to be difficult, and I'm sorry I can't show you around. Just search through the cupboards and fridge until you find things. Alice is coming later to make supper for us, and she will give you a guided tour." Lucie smiles and heads for the kitchen and I sink back into the pillows; this is so frustrating. How long am I supposed to stay here stuck in bed? Surely, I can have a shower, can't I?

It's not long before lunch arrives, a tray laden with chevre, olives, salad and crusty bread with a jug of lemonade. I smile and gesture for Lucie to pull up a chair and join me. "I hope this is okay," she says timidly, "I didn't know what you liked."

"It's perfect, thank you. I can eat most things, except goat," I laugh, then proceed to tell Lucie the story of Big Billy. It does the trick, and soon Lucie appears to relax, telling me a little about herself.

"I left my job in one of the prominent tourist hotels recently, as the shifts were long and punishing. I always had to cover as they were permanently short-staffed." Lucie pulls a face and shrugs her shoulders.

"Yes," I nod in understanding. "I used to be a nurse, and it was very similar, always being hounded to work extra shifts. I'm sorry that this was quite unexpected; we'll have to sort out a rota for you." Lucie nods as I continue, "It won't be difficult work. I'll contact Millie, the other lady that was interested; perhaps you could share the hours between yourselves."

After lunch, I ask Lucie to go back down to the kitchen to familiarise herself with the appliances as we have two guest rooms booked for tomorrow evening. The afternoon drags, and I try to keep myself occupied by answering emails and taking bookings for next year. I've decided not to take any more bookings for the next four weeks, but I'll have to somehow manage with the few guests who have already booked. By late afternoon, I'm incredibly bored and beginning to suffer cramps in my lower legs. That's it, I've had enough, and send Lucie a text.

Sorry to bother you, please could you come and give me a hand when you're free.

Within a minute, she knocks on my bedroom door and pokes her head in, "What can I do for you, Madam?"

"Please, call me Laura. I want to get out of bed and sit by the window. Could you arrange some cushions in the chair for me, please?" She nods and collects several cushions and places them in the chair then walks back over to me, looking apprehensive. "Don't worry," I say. "I'm not expecting you to lift me, but I would appreciate you walking by my side, though, just in case."

Lucie looks uncertain and asks, "Are you sure?" I nod and smile as I shuffle my lumbering girth to sit on the side of the bed.

"Erm, Monsieur Besnard said I was to ring him if you tried to get out of bed," she adds, now looking uncomfortable.

"Oh, he did, did he?" She looks at me as though she's made a mistake, "Well, don't worry. I'll get back into bed before he arrives. Anyway, I'd like some fresh bedding, and you can't do that with me sat in bed. And I'll use the bathroom too." It feels fantastic to be back on my feet as I waddle to the bathroom with Lucie at my side. "Thank you. I'll be fine now."

When I return, she's already got my bed stripped. "Where will I find the clean bed linen?" Lucie asks, and I direct her to the linen cupboard. I try to get comfortable in my chair and look out of the window, purposefully avoiding watching Lucie make up my bed; I feel so useless not being able to help her. It's not long before another Braxton-Hicks contraction has me practising my breathing exercise, "Are you okay, shall I ring for Monsieur Besnard?" Lucy asks, looking concerned.

"No, thank you. It's nothing, and it will soon pass," I manage between breaths. I make a note of the time on my phone. I've only had four contractions so far today, and they're irregular. Noah must be feeling the squeeze too because he starts to move. Excellent, another tick on the kick chart that the midwife asked me to fill in. My phone rings with a number that I don't recognise. I answer hesitantly, "Hello?"

"Hello, it's Millie, sorry I missed your call."

"Millie, thank you for getting back to me," I say. "Unfortunately, I'm on bed rest at the moment and was wondering if you might be able to help out with some light duties?" I go on to explain my predicament, and Millie agrees to work with Lucie to cover some days over the next week; that's an enormous relief.

45

The days begin to blend into one, and I've lost count of how long I've been in my bedroom. Thankfully, the midwife has now agreed that I can take frequent short walks around my room and use the bathroom facilities. Shadow is as ever, my faithful companion, that is when he's not out looking for truffles with Xavier, Patch, and Pepper. We have a bumper harvest and Xavier and Gus are taking them to market tomorrow. When Xavier comes up to bed, I ask, "Have you got everything ready for morning?"

"Yes, ze truck is packed. All I 'ave to do is pick up Gus and ze dog in ze morning."

"Why are you taking Beau with you?"

"I'm not. Pepper is coming wiz us."

"Why? Won't he be better off here at the Chateau?"

"When zey see 'ow good 'e is at finding truffles, 'e will fetch an 'igh price," he says, rubbing his hands.

I sit up quickly and look at him, horrified. "You can't sell him now," I protest. "He's one of the family!" My movement has the effect of initiating another contraction, and once again, I'm forced to sit back and begin to concentrate on my breathing.

Xavier's features soften, and he puts his hand on my shoulder. When the contraction subsides, he sits beside me and takes hold of my hand, "You must not get upset; it's not good for you or ze baby."

"Not get upset!" I demand, removing my hand from his. "How can I not get upset when you say things like that. We are not selling Pepper!" He looks at me and opens his mouth to speak, then hesitates and shakes his head. Curious, I ask, "What were you about to say?"

"Nozing, it's not important."

"Well, I think it is."

He sighs then says, "You knew zat we were going to sell 'im—"

"But you've said yourself how good he is at finding truffles," I interrupt. "Why don't we keep him and then we'll have even more truffles to sell?"

Xavier looks at me and sighs again. "Laura, we already 'ave Shadow and Patch to find ze truffles. Why would we need anozer dog?"

"Gus could learn! He could be Gus's dog."

"No. Gus is responsible for Patch. Ze boy is getting quite good wiz 'im."

Okay, this isn't working. Time for plan B. "How much are you selling him for?"

"One zousand Euros," he replies with a grin.

"Deal," I say, staring hard into his face.

"What is ze deal?"

"One thousand Euros. I'll buy him from you for one thousand Euros."

Once more, his features soften, and he retakes my hand, "Laura. First of all, ze dog is already yours; I'm selling 'im on your behalf…"

"Okay, the decision's made," I say then lean over to Xavier's ear and exclaim, "he is not for sale!" Before he gets a chance to reply, I bend forwards as another contraction travels through my abdomen.

Xavier looks on worriedly. "Laura, zis conversation is over; you need to calm down."

I begin breathing and count to twenty, but it doesn't subside as it has previously. I continue counting and get to thirty-six before it improves, and I flop back into the pillows.

"Can I get you anyzing?"

"Water, please." Xavier hands me a glass of water, and I take a big gulp.

Twenty minutes later and Xavier is asleep; how can he fall asleep so easily? The minutes tick by. Half-an-hour goes by, and I'm still wide awake, so I lean down to get my tablet off the floor. That was a big mistake. Another contraction begins, taking my breath away. "Ow, ow, ow!" I yelp and try to breathe my way through it, but it's worse than the one before, and my back is so uncomfortable. I roll onto my side and try to sit on the edge of the bed, but it's almost impossible. At last, the pain subsides, and I manage to heave myself up to a standing position, which feels a little more comfortable, except for the fact that I feel like I've got a rugby ball between my legs. Toilet, perhaps I need a wee. I waddle over to the bathroom and put the light on as a gush of water leaves my body. Damn! I didn't get here in time. I look at the puddle that I'm standing in when reality dawns — my waters have broken — this is it. Labour. I'm going to meet my son tomorrow. A searing pain swiftly wipes the smile off my face, and I stand on my tiptoes to try to get away from it, but it doesn't work. *Breathe Laura, breathe.* The contraction seems to last for an age, and I eventually lean forward with relief and grab hold of the washbasin as it disappears.

Okay, this is it, the real deal. I need to get to the hospital. I clean myself up and shuffle back into the bedroom, looking for something suitable to wear. "What are you doing?" Xavier asks groggily. I don't have time to answer as yet another gripping pain takes over and I bend forwards and wail as it reaches a crescendo. Xavier is beside me before I can straighten up, "Laura, is ze baby coming?" I try to straighten, but the pain still has me in its grip, and I nod, unable to speak. "Merde! What do you need me to do?"

"Get rid of this pain!" I wail, dropping onto all fours and gasping for breath.

Xavier puts the light on and runs his fingers through his hair, his facial muscles twitch, then set hard, and he throws his hands up in the air as panic strikes, "I don't know what to do!"

"Alice, get Alice," I manage to gasp as the pain, at last, dissipates. "Ring the hospital too." I curl up on the floor as I hear Xavier talking on the phone.

He approaches and crouches by my side, "Zey want to talk to you." Xavier holds the phone to my ear, and I take it from him.

The emergency operator asks, "How many weeks pregnant are you?"

"Thirty-seven as of tomorrow," I huff.

"How often are the contractions?" I drop the phone and scream as another searing pain feels as though it's tearing me in two.

Xavier picks the phone up and speaks rapidly in French; most of which I don't take in. "Zey

are sending an ambulance," he says, looking
horrified.

"Where's Alice?" I huff, between breaths.

"She isn't answering ze phone; she sleeps like
an 'ibernating bear. Merde!"

 "Help me to sit up," I say, as the pain
recedes, like a wave on the shore, and the
tension leaves my body. Xavier looks relieved
to be doing something and does as I ask
assisting me onto the bed. "Towels. Get lots
of towels," I snap, gesturing with my arms.
He returns swiftly with the new, white, fluffy
towels that I've bought for the guest rooms.
I'm about to scold him further when another
contraction takes the words out of my mouth.
"Where is that bloody ambulance?" I wail
through gritted teeth. "I need pain relief!"
This contraction lasts longer and is far worse
than the previous ones. "Jenny," I gasp. "Get
Jenny on Skype." Xavier stands and looks at
me as though he hasn't heard my barked

instruction. "Now!" I shout, which seems to work.

A few minutes later, I'm looking into the eyes of my best friend. "Oh my God!" Jenny's voice says while she peers out of the screen.

"Help! Jenny. Please. It's unbearable!" I moan in-between pants.

"Claire!" Jenny shouts. "Claire! Get in here. Now!" She looks over her shoulder. "Just a minute!" She says to me as her face disappears off-screen.

"Don't leave me…" I shout, then Claire's face appears on my screen.

"Claire's now a midwife, she'll help you," I hear Jenny shout in the background.

"Okay, we can do this. You're thirty-seven weeks, right?" I nod. "Good, any complications?" I shake my head, then Xavier appears at my side and tells her about my week of bed rest. "When did baby last move?"

"Erm, a couple of hours ago. Whoa!" I moan as my body is racked by another contraction, "Oh, no! No!"

Claire asks, "What's wrong, Laura?"

"Push! I need to push!"

Xavier looks at me, and his features freeze in terror. "But. Err. Merde! You can't 'ave ze baby 'ere!"

"Oh yes, she can. Let's do this. Right, Xavier go and wash your hands and come right back, do you hear?" He nods with his mouth wide open and stares at the screen in shock, "Now! Do it now!" He leaps off the bed and returns quickly.

"Need to push this thing out of me. Now!" I scream, which makes Xavier jump, and his face blanches.

"Xavier, listen to me, I need you to, very gently, feel for Laura's cervix and tell me what it feels like." He looks at me aghast then back at the screen. Claire nods encouragingly at him. "You can do it, go on. Wait until the contraction stops then very gently feel."

My body sags when the pain retreats, but Xavier doesn't move. "Now, do it now, please," I wail. He steps forward and slowly and gently puts his hand between my legs.

Claire asks, "Well?"

"I don't know what I'm feeling for."

"Okay, a normal cervix feels a bit like a nose."

"No, no nose."

"What can you feel Xavier?"

"A 'ole."

"Okay, does this hole have any edges, like the rim of a jam-jar?"

"Erm, no, just a 'ole, and slime. Ooh, 'air, I can feel some 'air!" He shouts, withdrawing his hand.

"Good man. Now, have you got a torch? Your phone. Use the light from your phone and put the laptop between Laura's legs so I can see."

The laptop disappears from view between my legs and I can no longer see Claire but can hear her muffled voice giving Xavier instructions. My heart rate spikes and sweat trickles down my face as fear grabs me. What if this goes wrong? What if Noah needs assistance with his breathing? What if… Pain takes over again, and everything else blurs around the edges. Somewhere in my periphery I hear, "Push Laura! Push, ze baby is coming!" I try to remember the instructions from the DVD that I watched about giving birth and drop my chin to my chest, take a deep breath and push down hard with every fibre of my being. "Good girl," Xavier echoes. My battered body relaxes once again, and I wipe away the sweat that's running into my eyes. However, respite is brief as the pain takes over once more. This time it feels different — I feel invigorated — and take a deep breath, a sense of calm washing over me.

I can do this. *Think of Noah*, I tell myself, will he be feeling discomfort too?

"Good girl, you're doing fantastically well," I hear Claire shout, followed by Xavier repeating her words; he appears at my side briefly then disappears back to the business end. Time seems to stand still as contraction after contraction follows and I push with every ounce of energy that I possess. "Nearly there now" filters into my brain.

"I need a rest now. Please. Can't we stop and carry on in the morning?" I protest.

"What? It isn't like zat. You 'ave to do zis, and now. Zen you can sleep," I hear Xavier say. Sleep, yes, sleep. I relax. Two minutes later, the next contraction rolls over me. Xavier encourages, "Zis is it Laura, one more push." I lean forward and push until it feels like my insides are dropping out. Meanwhile, a burning, stinging sensation begins. I moan and wail, but Xavier gives me no time for self-pity. "Pant!" He orders, "Pant, now, like ze dog." An image of Shadow with his long, pink tongue hanging out pops into my head and I pant as instructed. The pain is excruciating, and I scream. "Good girl, push Laura, one more push!" I don't need telling twice as the overwhelming sensation takes over and I give one final push. "Ze 'ead is out, 'e 'as lots of black curly 'air!"

"Is it over?" I ask. I can hear Xavier talking, but to whom?

"It's nearly over, one or two more pushes zen Noah will be 'ere. You can do it."

"I can do it. I can do it," I chant as I lean forward and push my son into the world.

"It's 'ere, ze baby is 'ere," Xavier says, gently placing Noah on my belly while he wipes the mucus away from his face; just like he did when delivering the lambs. I can only see Noah's head and chest. Then, his tiny hands come into view as he lifts them and begins to cry.

"Noah, my darling boy, hello," I whisper to the top of his black curly hair.

Xavier comes to my side and places a soft kiss on my lips, "Zank you, zank you. You were amazing." I look into his eyes to see tears spilling down his cheeks.

"Can I hold my son?"

Xavier picks our baby up and places it in my arms. He looks at me and his features melt into the softest smile, "No, but you can 'old our daughter."

The world stands still as I look down to see that I am indeed holding our daughter, my Sweet Pea. She stops crying, and I begin. The flood gates open as tears blur my vision. Xavier wipes them away and places a kiss on my lips, followed by one on our daughter's small, bloody cheek, "I love you so much, both of you; my amazing girls."

Xavier brings the laptop back for me to see Claire and Jenny beaming at me through the miles. "Congratulations, you were both marvelous, now where's that bloody ambulance?" Jenny growls.

EPILOGUE
TWO AND A HALF YEARS LATER

I'm sitting on the balcony with my breakfast
tray at the beginning of yet another hectic day.
We're attending a summer wedding. Alice has
arrived with her husband, Monsieur Le Maire,
but I'm now allowed the considerable
privilege of calling him Charles, well, at least
in private. Alice is busy dressing Flora, our
beautiful little girl. She looks so much like her
father and big brother, Gus. I take another
moment to admire the view, one that I'll
never tire of before getting dressed too. My
life is so blessed. I have a fantastic home here
in the attic of our Chateau. Adam has done a
brilliant job.

Alice pops her head out onto the balcony.
"I'm taking Flora down now. See you soon." I
follow her inside and hug my darling little girl,
she grins and does a twirl in her pretty dress

before her grandmother takes her hand and heads downstairs.

Charles clears his throat and puts a hand on my shoulder, "I'll go down and make myself useful. Breakfast service should be over by now." I smile and nod gratefully. These people have taken me to their heart. I'm incredibly fortunate. So many of the locals are here to help with the event. Both Lucie and Millie are here today. Lucie is helping Sylvie, Rose, and Yvette with the catering and Millie is on childcare duty, so I can be free to mingle with the guests.

Jenny, who's here for a week, greets me at the bottom of the stairs. I'm amazed that she's up before me. "Everyone is in the marquee, shall we?"

I nod and follow her out of the door into the brilliant sunshine. As we approach, I hear the piano start to play. Gus has been practising the piece for ages now and has it off to perfection. He's such a talented young man.

The marquee flaps open, and I step inside. It's an image of perfection. Sweet peas decorate the whole interior, and the scent is delightful. Flora runs up to me carrying a basket of flowers and hugs me, then she holds my hand and walks by my side. I can see Xavier. He's tried his best and is wearing a suit and tie. I wonder who he borrowed them from.

"Who gives this woman away?" Monsieur Le Maire asks. Jenny steps forward and nods. "Do you, Laura Mackley, take Xavier Besnard to be your lawful husband?"

I turn to look at the man beside me, and my heart melts as I remember all of the things that we've been through together. "I do." I take his hand and continue, "I promise to fall in love with you more with each passing day and to put you and our children at the centre of my world." Xavier looks deep into my soul, and I have to catch my breath before continuing, "I promise to put you before all others and honour you, but not obey; because that's a little creepy. Oh, and don't ever kill one of my goats again!"

Xavier throws his head back and laughs heartily, and our friends join him. When the laughter subsides, I step back because now it's his turn. "I promise to cherish and 'onour you until death do us part. And love you and our children at all times, even in ze truffle season." He pauses and waits for the laughter to stop then adds, "In ze storybook of our lives, zis is ze part where I promise to you zat we will live 'appily ever after."

THE END

***

I hope you have enjoyed following Laura and Xavier on their exciting journey.

I would be extremely grateful if you would consider leaving me a review. Reviews from readers are really important to a self-published

author as Amazon directly relates the number
of reviews to the position on the listings
which appear when customers do a search.

***

www.emma-sharp-author.com

ABOUT THE AUTHOR

Emma Sharp is the author of The Chateau Trilogy comprising of: The Letter, Sweet Pea and Secrets and Surprises. She is currently working on her latest novel, Innocence in Provence, which will be available in late 2020.

Emma, a former nurse was born and raised in Yorkshire. She has two grown up daughters, a grand-daughter and a much-loved French Bulldog, Nellie. She loves to travel and finds that she writes her best work when she's at her caravan amidst the stunning scenery of the Yorkshire Dales.

She has also appeared on local radio reading her short stories and is as a member of a writing group, who meet regularly to review and appraise each other's work.

I hope you enjoy reading her novels.